# GENEVER

## 500 YEARS OF
## HISTORY IN A BOTTLE

*Véronique Van Acker - Beittel*

FLEMISH LION

Cover photo National Genever Museum, Hasselt, Belgium
Cover design by Christine Janaske
Edited by JP Ishaq

ISBN: 0615795854
ISBN-13: 978-0-615-79585-0

# GENEVER

## 500 YEARS OF
## HISTORY IN A BOTTLE

# CONTENTS

# PREFACE

Genever [juh-nee-ver] is the national spirit of Belgium and the Netherlands with a fascinating history spanning six centuries. First distilled in Flanders during the 16th century, where it was used for medicinal purposes, the evolution of genever is well-preserved in manuscripts, artifacts, paintings, pictures, and tradition.

Driven by wars and a 17th century distilling ban that lasted over a century, Flemish distillers and their genever migrated throughout Holland, France, and Germany. The Dutch absorbed much of the genever trade into their well-established commerce system, shipping it around the world. Eventually the British used genever as an inspiration for creating what is known today as gin. During the 19th century, genever received an early place at the American cocktail bar. Many classic gin cocktails were originally made with genever. While the Americans were imbibing genever cocktails, Belgian distillers benefitted greatly from the Industrial Revolution and genever production reached unprecedented heights leading to the creation of a new style of genever. In the early 20th century, Belgian genever struggled through another difficult period as distilleries were completely stripped of copper during World War I by occupying German forces, which they melted down for artillery shell casings. This nearly ground traditional genever production to a halt, almost ending a national tradition.

In addition to the struggles created by the war, in 1919 a 66 year ban was placed on serving genever in Belgian bars. This radical law was enacted as an answer to excessive liquor consumption. Although this ban hurt Belgian genever, it led to the popularity of Belgian beer as we know it today. Dutch genever escaped the war and didn't experience the same ban that Belgium suffered and continued to grow in popularity leading to the common misconception that genever is a Dutch creation.

Genever's colorful past has earned this historic spirit a *Protected Designation of Origin* that pertains to any genever distilled in Belgium, the Netherlands and small parts of France and Germany. Genever is a strictly European regulated distilled beverage with many protected classes and types, of which most are exclusive to Belgium.

Around the world, the Belgians are known for their world-class beers. While beer may be Belgium's most widespread alcoholic export, genever has been the country's national and traditional spirit for over five hundred years.

I was born and raised in East-Flanders, the Flemish region of Belgium. I first tried genever as a teenager at a Christmas market in Bruges, the largest city of West-Flanders, Belgium's Flemish region. Christmas markets are an essential part of the holiday season and feature tiny A-frame chalets set up around ice skating rinks. These markets offer Christmas decorations, Belgian waffles and, of course, genever. Genever is served chilled in an hourglass-shaped shot glass filled to the brim. This makes it impossible to pick up the glass without spilling, so tradition dictates that people take their first sip without using their hands. Then, with the genever safe from spilling, patrons raise their glasses in a toast, saying *"Gezondheid!"* Experiencing this tradition firsthand in my youth ignited my fascination with genever.

In 2002, I emigrated to the United States and began a career as a marketing professional working for Fortune 500 companies in Trade and Strategic Marketing. Several years later, I fell in love with an American boy, Matthew, and in 2007 we were married in Belgium. The day before the ceremony, I organized a tour of my college town, Ghent, for our American guests. We ended our city visit at 't Dreupelkot, an internationally renowned genever bar tucked away in Ghent's historic, medieval city center. 'T Dreupelkot serves only genever, but with over 200 different Belgian varieties, that's hardly a limitation. It is served in shot glasses filled to the brim in the traditional way, making it the perfect spot to introduce Belgium's national drink to my wedding guests, just the way I remembered it.

For our American guests it was their first taste of genever, and we quickly graduated from ordering shots to full bottles, trying every kind we could. Eventually my father told me it was time to come home so he would have someone to walk down the aisle the next day. I went, but I never forgot what it was like to witness my new American family's discovery of genever, and how it helped me recapture the joy of experiencing that spirit for the first time.

Years after the wedding, the Americans continued to ask about this delectable, mysterious spirit I had introduced them to, and if I could bring some back from my next visit to Belgium. Lugging genever back to the US was something I had already done many times, but now I needed to find a way to get real volume through customs. I missed my homeland and genever in particular, and I wanted to bring those parts of my life to the US. It became clear to me that there was a way to reconnect with my heritage and share my love of genever with the untapped American market: I would import it myself.

I was inspired to quit my corporate job and founded Flemish Lion LLC, establishing the first company in America's history to import Belgian genever. It's been a significant endeavor with plenty of challenges, as I've had to teach myself about importing, the liquor business, and the process of establishing an entirely new liquor category, but it's given me the opportunity to fall more and more in love with the Belgian liquor I grew up with. Genever is near and dear to me; more than just a drink, it truly is the spirit of Belgium and it is one worth sharing with friends and family. This book is my way of sharing my passion, not to mention all the research and knowledge I've acquired, in the hope that others will come to appreciate genever as I have.

# 13<sup>TH</sup> TO 16<sup>TH</sup> CENTURIES: GENEVER'S EARLY HISTORY

*Genever is the national and traditional spirit of Belgium and the Netherlands. As with any culturally integral food or drink, its history and its character are intricately tied to the soil and water from which it grows.*

The origin of genever can be traced back to the Middle Ages, when alchemists in the Low Countries used the distilled drink for medicinal purposes. The Low Countries are the lands around the low-lying delta of three key rivers carved through Northern Europe: the Rhine, the Scheldt, and the Meuse. Today, these rivers, linked by an extensive network of shipping canals and waterways, wind around modern day Belgium, the Netherlands, Luxembourg, and parts of France and Germany.

Belgium's centralized location led to its being the site of innumerable battles between neighboring European powers and earning it the designation of the "cockfighting arena" of Europe. This intricate history and the resulting cultural cross-pollination have given Belgium three official languages: Dutch, French, and German, as well as three relatively autonomous regions: Flanders in the north, Wallonia in the south, and Brussels, located between the two. The Flemish who inhabit Flanders, a flatland crisscrossed by canals, speak Dutch. "Dutch" generally refers to the language as a whole, and the Belgian dialects are often collectively referred to as Flemish. The southern Walloons, in the rolling hills of Wallonia, speak French and the centrally located Brussels is officially bilingual. German is the least prevalent official language in Belgium, spoken natively by less than 1% of the population.

The national language of Belgium's northern neighboring and panoramic tulip country, the Netherlands, inhabited by the Dutch, is also Dutch. The term Holland is frequently used to refer to the whole of the Netherlands even though Holland itself is only a small region in the western part of the country.

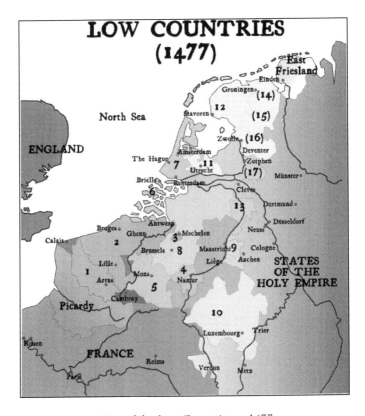

*Map of the Low Countries c. 1477*
*The Low Countries are numbered (a total of 17 Provinces)*
The Seventeen Provinces, a term applied in the 15th and 16th
century, roughly covered the Low Countries, i.e. the current
Netherlands, Belgium, Luxembourg, a good part of the North
of France (Artois, French Flanders), and a small part of
Western Germany.

Unlike wine and beer, which were recreationally imbibed in Europe, distilled drinks were originally the tools of healers and made primarily for medicinal purposes. The center of alchemical knowledge in Flanders, Belgium during the Middle Ages was the city of Bruges.

During the 13th and 14th century, Bruges was the most important center of international trade at the North Sea. From all parts of the world, products like wool, gold, spices, steel, leather and silk arrived at this port and were traded with the English, French, Germans, Italians and other tradesmen in the Low Countries. Alchemists flocked to this port area, finding every herb and medicinal plant they needed to craft their potions and elixirs. A wealth of recovered manuscripts show that alchemy in Flanders was not practiced solely by would-be magicians trying to transform lead into gold or create the fabled philosopher's stone. Alchemy was primarily practiced by merchants trying to come up with distillations from which to isolate medical oils.

Genever owed much of its healing properties to the use of juniper berries, which were widely available and a popular ingredient in remedies at the time. Juniper berries grow on the juniper tree, a small shrub widely distributed throughout the Northern Hemisphere. The berries take two or three years to ripen and a single plant holds berries in every stage of ripeness. Only the ripe blue berries are picked for their volatile oil, which is most abundant just before the peak ripeness and darkening of the fruit.

Juniperus communis L.

*Drawing of the entire juniper plant*
Alchemists used juniper in distillations from which to
isolate medical oils. Genever owed much of its healing
properties to the use of juniper berries.

The first written reference to genever was by Flemish poet Jacob van Maerlant in his twelve-part encyclopedia, *Der Naturen Bloeme*. The tome, focusing on European flora and fauna, was written in rhyme in Damme, an outlying port of Bruges, between 1266 and 1269. According to Van Maerlant's verse, bathing in rainwater boiled with juniper berries was a good remedy to cure stomach aches, and juniper berries boiled in wine was recommended for intestinal pains. The latter drink is the precursor of genever as we know it today.

*Jeghen buuc evel van leden*
*So salmen jenewere sieden*
*In reynwatre ende dat ontfaen.*
*Die met lancevel es bevaen*
*Siede jenewer in wine,*
*Ets goet jegen sine pine.*

In various editions of *Der Naturen Bloeme*, genever is written as jenevere, jenewer, jenewere, jenieveren, genever, genevere or genevre. Even today we can still write *jenever* (Dutch for juniper), *genièvre* (French for juniper) or *genever* (the old Dutch spelling that is in common English usage), a name derived from the juniper berry, genever's key botanical and medicinal ingredient. Van Maerlant was the first to note the combination of juniper berries with wine and can be credited for recording genever's first known predecessor.

*Badend meisje (bathing girl)*
*Girl bathing in rainwater in which juniper berries were cooked*
Bathing in water with juniper berries was believed
to have medicinal powers.

Later, in the mid 14<sup>th</sup> century, the outbreak of plague or 'Black Death' in the Low Countries would kill off nearly a third of Europe's population in just four years. This necessitated the use of "distilled waters" to prevent the spread of disease. The distillation of medicinal water was an Arab discovery, particularly rose water, a product distilled from freshly picked rose petals which was used as both a perfume and a medicine. Arab medical wisdom at that time had been disseminated across Europe via universities and monasteries.

In the Low Countries, it was primarily the Cistercian monasteries in the area surrounding Bruges that catalogued this knowledge. It is therefore not coincidental that the oldest known text in the Low Countries concerning alcohol was written in this same area: a manuscript that has been preserved in the Royal Library of Brussels. The author is unknown but believed by dialect experts to be from West-Flanders. In 1351, the manuscript was copied by Flemish alchemist Johannes van Aalter.

The text explains how one can distill wine in a 20-liter alembic. The author names this distilled medicine *aqua vitae* or water of life. *Aqua vitae* was believed to be capable of preventing and curing a wide range of ailments from the plague to gray hair and even aging. Crushing different sorts of berries, seeds and herbs into it allegedly further increased its palliative powers. But one of the most important benefits of *aqua vitae* was that "it makes people forget human sorrow" and makes "the heart glad and strong and courageous." Initially, this healing concoction was to be taken in drop form; as a result of these euphoric properties, within a century this stimulant had become a drink for pleasure, and the typical dosage had somehow grown to a full shot. This popular people's drink was named *brandewijn*, or burned wine (brandy).

Many other books about "distilled waters" followed, but one publication in particular, *Een Constelijck Distileerboec*, written in Antwerp, Flanders, Belgium, played a major role in the distilling history of the Low Countries. It's not coincidental that the distillation knowledge had now shifted from the Bruges area to Antwerp. In the 1490s, as Bruges' waterways to the sea gradually silted up, trade shifted further north and Antwerp, with a network of roads connecting it to Germany, had emerged as the pre-eminent commercial city in the region. This shining center of commerce quickly became a spiritual and intellectual hub of communication and information, and even important humanists like Erasmus and Thomas Moore began to send their manuscripts to printers in Antwerp. During this period, Antwerp was the richest city of Europe.

In 1552, Philippus Hermanni, a physician in Antwerp, penned *Een Constelijck Distileerboec*, a book on distilling including the preparation method of *geneverbessenwater* ("juniper berry water") or *genever aqua* vitae ("genever water of life"). In Hermanni's *geneverbessenwater* method, credited as the first printed genever recipe, juniper berries were crushed, sprinkled with wine, and then distilled in an alembic. Hermanni describes how the juniper berry water can be consumed for digestive disorders, colds, plague, and bites of venomous animals.

Hermanni also referred to "spirits" or "forces of wine" which are driven out by heat, marking the first time in Dutch literature that alcoholic vapor was tied to spirits. His text was such a success that it was reprinted in 1558, 1566 and 1570 in Antwerp and eventually in Amsterdam, Holland, the Netherlands in 1612 and 1622. *Een Constelijck Distileerboec* was considered the manual for distillers for many years, contributing to the explosive growth of the malt spirit industry in the Low Countries.

*Alembic for the production of geneverbessenwater (juniper berry water) as shown in Een Constelijck Distileerboec, Antwerp, Flanders, Belgium, 1552*

*Painting of the unloading of wine barrels from a ship with the help of manpower and a crane in 16<sup>th</sup> century Bruges, Flanders, Belgium*

Barrels of wine arrived at numerous ports in the Low Countries to keep up with the growing demand for distillations from wine.

Around the same time, the rising popularity of *brandewijn*, or brandy, distilled from wine suffered due to consecutive bad vineyard harvests from 1511-1524 and cold waves in 1540 and onwards. As grapes grew scarce, wine grew more expensive. Distillers are both artists as well as businessmen; they knew they needed to find less expensive ingredients to make their popular drink more affordable for themselves to produce and for consumers to purchase. They began to distill *brandewijn* from unclear or murky beer instead of wine.

Towards the end of the 16th century, this type of distillation had become so popular that it was no longer distilled from beer but from a fermented grain mash of rye and malted barley. This grain mash received the name *moutwijn* or "malt wine." The malt spirit produced from this grain mash or malt wine was called *korenbrandewijn* or "cereal/grain brandy" and was eventually shortened to *korenwijn* or "cereal/grain wine."

Today *korenwijn* is often incorrectly translated into English as corn wine, as corn was not even present in this spirit and would not be used in the Low Countries by distillers until 1878. Additionally, the Dutch word for corn is *mais*, while the English translation for *koren* is cereal/grain. *Koren* is a general term for grain cultivated for food. Depending on the region it may refer to rye, wheat, or barley.

Although it was much cheaper to distill from grain rather than wine, the resulting spirit was not a sophisticated drink, and constant experimentation was carried out to find a way of improving the quality and flavor. Juniper berries combined well with malt wine, were prevalent in the Low Countries, and were already widely incorporated in a number of remedies; however, another benefit juniper provided to the alcoholic drink was making it more palatable and thus easier to sell to the general population for consumption. People started calling this tasty concoction of malt wine and juniper berries by its distinguishing feature: genever (Dutch for juniper). In the Low Countries from this time on, genever became the people's drink. A new industry – distilled drinks for recreational use – was born.

*Moutwijn (malt wine) in barrels*
During the 16<sup>th</sup> century, genever, a concoction of malt wine and juniper berries, became the people's drink.

The exact moment at which juniper berries were first used to flavor malt wine is one of history's great mysteries, leaving us to wonder just who first crafted genever. Just as Poland and Russia continue to battle over the lineage of vodka, the heritage of genever comes down to two countries: Belgium and the Netherlands.

A common but controversial theory credits French-Flemish Dr. Sylvius de Bouve also known as Dr. Franciscus Sylvius de la Boë (1614-1672), a medical doctor and professor at the University of Leyden in Holland, the Netherlands. According to legend, the professor first manufactured genever while researching a cure for stomach and kidney disorders. Curiously, just as word of this phenomenal new medicine spread throughout Leyden and the surrounding countryside, the population experienced a surge in kidney and stomach disorders. Demand was so great that Dr. Sylvius found it difficult to keep his medicine in stock. He needed to produce genever in larger quantities and at a faster pace. Historians surmise that Dr. Sylvius struck an agreement with local distillers to help bring his drink to the masses.

The problem with this theory is that during Dr. Sylvius's fourteen-year tenure as a professor at the University of Leyden, his research included distilling medicines with juniper berry oil, but none of his research papers contain any reference to genever. The dates also don't add up: Dr. Sylvius certainly wasn't the first to distill with juniper or call a concoction genever, as proven by written references to genever in 13th century Bruges, Flanders (*Der Naturen Bloeme*) and 16th century Antwerp, Flanders (*Een Constelijck Distileerboec*).

Additionally, in 1606 the Dutch had already levied taxes on genever and similar liquors which were sold as alcoholic drinks, suggesting that genever had stopped being seen as a medicinal remedy many years before Dr. Sylvius was even born. Genever's prevalence can also be observed in Massinger's 1623 play, "The Duke of Milan", which references "geneva" (see excerpt on page 32). Geneva was the Anglicized name for genever, which British soldiers had brought back with them upon returning from battle in the Low Countries in 1587 and again during the early 1600's. Dr. Sylvius would have been just nine years old when Massinger's play opened. So while the legend of Dr. Sylvius's "medicine" may be more myth than fact, it has become the tale most people know.

The nature of the world in the 15th and 16th century, at least in western Europe, was that only the wealthy had ready access to books, manuscripts, or enough education to become literate; the majority of people, including alchemists, relied on oral tradition for the transmission of knowledge. Juniper was a widely available and common adjunct at the time, added to various distillations or potions, and alchemy was widespread and practiced by many. History is rarely tidy enough to offer one responsible author for a new discovery. There remains no definitive proof from either Belgium or the Netherlands as to who invented genever but we can unambiguously claim that the early history of genever lies in Flanders, Belgium.

*Present day Flanders shown within Belgium
and neighboring countries*

# 17<sup>TH</sup> CENTURY:
## GENEVER CONQUERS THE WORLD

*A distilling ban in Belgium allows Dutch genever to conquer the world.*

Resulting from a distilling ban in Belgium, a Flemish distiller migration spread their knowledge and practices throughout the Netherlands, France, and Germany. The Dutch, who were spared the crackdown, absorbed much of the genever trade into their own well-established commerce system, shipping it around the world. Eventually, they introduced genever to the British, who turned genever into gin.

In the early 17th century, the population of the Southern Low Countries (comprising the majority of modern day Belgium) suffered its own version of Prohibition. And like American Prohibition, it resulted in a domino effect, the consequences of which can still be observed today. Meager grain harvests had become the norm during the 17th century, and the numerous occupying armies traversing the region often consumed what little grain was left, to the great dismay of farmers. Wars caused restricted trade, famine, and various epidemics, so it should have come as no surprise that many people drowned their suffering with beer and genever.

In 1601, Archduke Albrecht and Archduchess Isabella, rulers of the Southern Low Countries, expressed growing concerns about the amount of grain being used for distilling alcohol. The government believed that grain was to be used for baking bread and worried about a national food shortage. As a result, they issued a ban on the production of spirits distilled from grain and fruit. In response, some distillers toiled on illegally, but many packed their pots and fled the country for more welcoming territories.

Many had already fled at the beginning of the Eighty Years' War (1568-1648) which began as a religious, political, and financial revolt of the Low Countries, one of the richest regions of Europe, against the powerful Spanish. The *Val van Antwerpen* or Fall of Antwerp in 1585 is often seen as a crucial and traumatic turning point in the history of relations between the Southern and Northern Low Countries, what would become Belgium and the Netherlands. When the siege of Antwerp began, most of Flanders and Brussels had been captured in the preceding year. With my dark brown hair and dark brown eyes, I'm walking evidence of the Spanish conquest.

At the time, Antwerp was not only the largest Dutch-speaking city but was also the cultural, economic, and financial center of the Low Countries. Antwerp was the period's *de facto* capital of Northern Europe. The city lay on the Scheldt River just inland from the English Channel, and was able to weather the siege as long as shipping was possible. However, in February 1585 the Spanish constructed a 730-meter (0.45 miles) bridge of ships on the Scheldt River, and the starvation of the city began. On August 17, 1585, Antwerp, crippled by the blockade of the Scheldt, surrendered. Of the pre-siege population of 100,000 people, only 40,000 remained.

Many of Antwerp's skilled tradesmen and the city's most dynamic thinkers migrated to the north, laying the commercial foundation for the subsequent "Dutch Golden Age." The Eighty Years' War shifted the center of prosperity from southern, Belgian cities such as Bruges, Antwerp, Ghent, and Brussels to the northern region (the modern day Holland, the Netherlands). For the next several centuries, the Dutch port of Amsterdam would play the dominant role in the region's trade.

*The Finis Bellis (Latin), Fin de la guerre (French) or End of War, a rebel ship employed during the siege of Antwerp against the Spanish forces c. 1585*

The Southern Low countries' loss of skilled distillers was their neighbors' gain: Today, Flemish distilleries can still be found in the Netherlands, France, and Germany, founded by the former owners of Flemish-established distilleries. Flemish distillers established the first distillery in Cognac, France, a reminder of which is the *Quai des Flamands* (The Flemish Dock), a dock along the Charente River in Cognac, where most of today's cognac distilleries reside.

The Southern Low Countries' distilling ban on grain and the resulting distiller migration left a hole in the genever market which was quickly filled by cities such as Hasselt (Flanders, Belgium) and Schiedam (Holland, the Netherlands) which lay outside Archduke Albrecht and Archduchess Isabella's territory and thus escaped the ban. Benefiting from the explosion of grain supply, available skilled tradesmen, and spiking demand, genever production in Hasselt and Schiedam soared. Even in the 21st century, Schiedam and Hasselt are still the genever capitals of the Netherlands and Belgium, respectively.

While the distillers of the Southern Low Countries (the Belgians) were still suffering the restraints of the ban on grain usage for the liquor industry, the Northern Low Countries (the Dutch) were hard at work and the 17th century became their Golden Age. Recognizing a good product and spared the ban, the 17th century sailors of the Dutch East India Company, or VOC, one of the first multinational corporations in the world, were the biggest consumers.

The sailors were entitled to ½ to 1 *mutsje* (75 to 150ml or 2.5 to 5 oz) of genever a day. A sailing trip to the East could take anywhere from nine months (with favorable winds) to two years, and sometimes it took even longer for ships to return. In a time before the convenience of refrigeration and frozen food, resupply was essential. The first place where new food and water could be purchased during the trip was *Kaap de Goede Hoop* (the Cape of Good Hope) in South Africa, a full four months' journey by ship from Holland. Preserving water and food, primarily fruit and vegetables, was an issue, causing a variety of illnesses for the sailors on board. Genever, believed to have medical powers, became a must for the crew on ships.

Genever turned out to be a valuable bartering commodity, too. Barrels of genever sailed across the seas to trading partners in all corners of the globe, including the Americas, West Africa, the Caribbean, and Argentina. Weighed down by corruption, the Dutch East India Company finally went bankrupt and closed its doors in 1799, while Dutch entrepreneurs took over the shipment of genever to the various Dutch colonies, as well as Britain, France, and the Americas.

*Dutch genever label for export to South-America c. 1910*
*Ginebra Legitima De Holanda*
*(Spanish for Genuine Holland Genever)*

# REGLEMENT

*Voor de Overheeden van de O. I. Compagnie Scheepen,*
*waar na dezelve haar in het verstrekken, of uitdee-*
*len der Victualien of Randsoenen voor 't Scheeps-*
*volk zullen hebben te reguleeren, als:*

### Zondags.

's morgens
- ¼ mutsje Genever aan ieder man.
- 1 kan Bier, zo lange het zelve goed is en strekken kan, voorts zo veel water de geheele weck door, en wel principaal tusschen de Keerkringen.
- 1 emmer Gort voor ieder 100 man.

's middags
- ¼ ℔ Vleesch voor ieder man; eerst de Schonken, zo lang dezelve strekken.
- 2 emmers Graauw Erwten voor ieder 100 man.
- 1 kleine bak Augurken voor ieder Baksvolk.
- 1 mutsje Wyn voor ieder man.

's avonds
- ½ mutsje Genever voor ieder man, en het overgebleeven Eeten.

### Maandag.

's morgens
- ¼ mutsje Genever voor ieder man.
- 1 emmer Gort voor ieder 100 man.

's middags
- 2 emmers Groene Erwten voor ieder 100 man.
- 25 ℔ Stokvis voor ieder 100 man.
- Peper, Mostert, Boter, tot sous maaken.

's avonds
- ½ mutsje Genever ieder man, en het overgebleeven Eeten.

### Dingsdag.

's morgens
- ½ mutsje Genever ieder man.
- 1 emmer Gort voor ieder 100 man.

's middags
- 2 emmers Witte Boonen voor ieder 100 man.
- ½ ℔ Spek voor ieder man.
- 1 kleine bak Augurken ieder Baksvolk.
- 1 mutsje Wyn ieder man.

's avonds
- ½ mutsje Genever ieder man, en het overgebleeven Eeten.

*A fragment from the regulation of the VOC in relation*
*to daily drinking – and food supplies, 18th century*
*'s morgens ½ mutsje Genever voor ieder man*
*'s avonds ½ mutsje Genever voor ieder man*
(in the morning 75ml Genever for every man,
in the evening 75ml Genever for every man)

*Poster in celebration of Distillery De Wildeman's 250th
anniversary, Amsterdam, Holland, the Netherlands c. 1914*
During the 17th century genever was traded around the globe
by the Dutch East India Company or VOC.

Genever not only traveled into pubs and houses across the globe, it also contributed to a slang term still in use today. In December 1585, Queen Elizabeth of England sent 6,000 men under the control of Robert Dudley, Count of Leicester to the Low Countries to provide support against the Spanish. The British soldiers arrived in Vlissingen, a harbor in the Northern Low Countries (the Netherlands) strategically located between the Scheldt River and the North Sea, before making their way to Antwerp.

Unfortunately, the British soldiers' brave attempt to save Antwerp from the siege and starvation came several months too late, but they did discover something new, observing a tradition among their Dutch counterparts. Before battle, the Dutch soldiers would sip from small bottles they kept on their belts. After these fortifying libations, the Dutch soldiers fought valiantly, passionately, and without fear. The English began to call this battle elixir "Dutch courage," a term which can still be heard today.

Two years later, Queen Elizabeth recalled the British soldiers to help secure peace between England and Spain. The British soldiers' separation from this newfound elixir was only a few battles away. At the outbreak of the Thirty Years' War (1618-1648), British and Dutch soldiers would fight side by side on the battlefield once more, gulping "Dutch courage" together again, at last.

During these wars, genever traveled from the battlefield to England, where it rose in popularity among the masses. It was Anglicized to "geneva", a term unrelated to the city of Geneva, the second largest city in Switzerland, but which sounded indistinguishable from [juh-nee-ver] to English ears.

Geneva was first referenced in English dramatist Massinger's 1623 play "The Duke of Milan."

Shown in following excerpt of "The Duke of Milan: A Tragedy (Scene I, Act I)", *Geneva print* has a twofold meaning, standing for *'in his cups'* (Geneva, a type of liquor) and for *'from the Bible'* (The Geneva Bible was one of the most historically significant translations of the Bible into the English language which took place in Geneva, Switzerland).

GRACCHO.

> *Take every man his flagon; give the oath*
> *To all you meet.*
> *I am this day the state-drunkard,*
> *I am, sure, against my will; and if you find*
> *A man at ten that's sober, he's a traitor,*
> *And in my name arrest him.*

JOVIO.

> *Very good, sir.*
> *But say he be a sexton?*

GRACCHO.

> *If the bells*
> *Ring out of tune, as if the streets were burning,*
> *And he cry ''Tis rare music', bid him sleep:*
> *'Tis a sign he has took his liquor; and if you meet*
> *An officer preaching of sobriety,*
> *Unless he read it in Geneva print,*
> *Lay him by the heels.*

JOVIO.

> *But think you 'tis a fault*
> *To be found sober?*

GRACCHO.

> *It is capital treason.*

*Arrival of Robert Dudley, Count of Leicester,*
*in Vlissingen, the Netherlands, c. 1585*
Two years later the Count and his soldiers returned to
England bringing "Dutch Courage" with them.

The recent arrival of the Dutch king, William of Orange, to the British throne in 1689 made genever (geneva) quite fashionable. Genever was now the drink of the king's court. It was hip, fashionable, and coveted. Genever also provided a tasty alternative to French brandy at a time of both political and religious tension between Britain and France. By 1690, the people of London were consuming 500,000 gallons of genever annually.

At the same time, some powerful landowners, eyeing a lucrative new market, pushed the 1690 Distilling Act through Parliament, allowing anyone to make spirits. Enterprising English distillers sought to produce their own version of the Dutch king's beloved spirit but struggled with the recipe. The rich, whisky-like malt wine was a challenge for the inexperienced distillers around London. With genever know-how and expertise tucked away in the Low Countries, the distillers had to improvise. So they eliminated the traditional malt wine and just mixed neutral grain alcohol with botanicals, often just soaked instead of being redistilled. Additionally, to save money on alcohol, distillers would dilute the mixture with things like turpentine, and cover their tracks with heavy juniper flavor.

Unable to match the complicated and time-consuming precision of the genever recipe, the resulting spirit was quite different, lacking the rich flavor of the malt wine but highlighting a much stronger juniper flavor. The wealthy needed a new term to distinguish the commoner's inferior liquor from their top-shelf imported genever. At the same time, English locals, finding genever and geneva too cumbersome to pronounce, gave their newly created liquor a shortened nickname: gin.

In 1702, William of Orange died of complications following a fall from his horse. William's death brought an end to the Dutch House of Orange and with it, an end to the English people's fascination with Dutch genever. The English gin industry exploded. The first style of gin to become popular was Old Tom Gin, a sweetened, grain-based, juniper-flavored spirit. This was followed by Plymouth Gin, a drier gin with a soft citrus character. Finally, London Dry emerged as the dominant style, and is now the world's most popular gin type, extremely dry and aromatic, and heavily flavored with juniper.

# 18<sup>TH</sup> CENTURY:
# DEMAND FOR GENEVER SOARS

*Belgium's distilling ban is lifted, farmers become home distillers, and the Dutch build the largest windmills in the world to keep up with the soaring demand of genever.*

After 112 years, the ban on distilling in the Southern Low Countries (comprising most of modern day Belgium) came to a swift end with the Habsburg family's ascent to power (1713-1794), encouraging distillers to dust off their stills and get back to work. However, Flemish farmers had set their sights beyond a stiff medicinal drink or two.

A byproduct of genever production was draff, a residue left over after the first distillation of the yeasted grain mash. Rich in proteins and cellulose, draff served as nutritious feed for cattle and pigs, keeping them healthy enough to survive harsh northern European winters. Closing the ecological circle, farmers used the manure from the animals to fertilize the agricultural fields for the grain crop, contributing to the next season's harvest and genever production.

Home distilleries on family farms, especially in East-Flanders, became commonplace. The farmers used large amounts of grain to distill genever, once again to the dismay of the local people. Whenever another grain shortage reared its head, they demanded the close of distilleries. The people's outcry fell on deaf ears with the farmers and the government. The farmers argued that not only bread but meat production also depended on the distilleries, and that if the pot stills stopped working, the draff that was used for fattening the cattle would vanish. The government argued that distilling created work for transporters, blacksmiths, as well as grain and coal traders. The income from the taxes levied against the farm distilleries was a convenient side-effect.

*Tax control at Notermans Distillery,*
*Hasselt, Flanders, Belgium c. 1900-1910*

The genever culture in the Northern Low Countries (comprising of modern-day Netherlands) continued to prosper in the 18th century. This is demonstrated by the proliferation of distilleries in the Schiedam area: in the beginning of the 18th century there were only 37 distilleries but by the end of the century, that number had exploded to 250. Schiedam had already become the go-to genever hub during the 17th century. A port city just outside of the Southern Low Countries, it had benefited from neighboring Belgium's 112-year distilling ban and genever production soared.

The smell of trouble wafted through Holland's largest distillery cities, Rotterdam and Amsterdam, would lead to the ultimate success of nearby Schiedam. The ever-increasing number of genever distilleries in those densely populated cities of Rotterdam and Amsterdam became a nuisance to the noses of the growing number of citizens. The smoking kettles, fueled by coal, caused air pollution, and the drinking water was contaminated by large amounts of water runoff from the distilleries. It's not for nothing that today's distilleries need to abide by strict environmental regulations.

When the miasma became unbearable, the miserable citizens asked the distillers to leave. Many did, setting up shop in Weesp, a town close to Amsterdam, and in Schiedam, a town close to Rotterdam. Soon, giant windmills appeared upon Schiedam's walls, milling the grains, a key ingredient for the swiftly multiplying genever distilleries. The growth brought with it an economic boom, as well as tremendous pollution from the coal-fueled distilleries, accompanied by open sewers, cholera epidemics, alcoholism, compounded by the abominable housing conditions of the laborers. Their work was hard and monotonous, the days were long, and their compensation was a pittance, forcing them to live in inner-city shanties, often crowding their large families into a single room.

The deteriorating conditions brought on by the genever boom swiftly earned Schiedam the nickname *Zwart Nazareth*, or Black Nazareth. The exact explanation behind the name has not been documented; however, it is known that the city walls and the houses were black (many of them remain black to this day). The coloration came from the billowing clouds of soot emitted by the distilleries, turning the city of narrow streets and allies into a coal-colored maze. But Nazareth? It was most likely a sarcastic reference to The Holy City, corrupted by pollution, alcoholism, and poverty.

At one point, Schiedam counted 25 windmills. To catch enough wind inside the city walls, the windmills were built to outsized proportions, becoming the tallest in the world. Five of the period's giant windmills still stand, proudly rotating their sails, their record heights unchallenged, including *Molen De Drie Koornbloemen*, Schiedam's oldest windmill, built in 1770. Recently, Schiedam completed the restoration of *Molen De Nieuwe Palmboom* (built in 1781), which was completed in 1993. The history of windmills in Schiedam is closely linked to that of genever. Tourists can visit this active traditional flour mill and climb all the way to the top, providing a stunning view of the other remaining windmills in the city.

*Schiedam, Holland, the Netherlands c. 1900*
Barrels of genever are waiting to get shipped around the world.

*De Drie Koornbloemen,*
*the oldest and highest windmill in the world still stands today*
*in Schiedam, Holland, the Netherlands*

# 19ᵀᴴ CENTURY:
# A NEW STYLE OF GENEVER

*Benefiting from the Industrial Revolution and the invention of the column still, genever production reaches unprecedented heights. A new day and style dawned for genever.*

Genever production in Belgium and the Netherlands soared in the 19th century, benefiting from the Industrial Revolution. Belgium was one of the first industrialized countries of Europe thanks to its geographic location between the industrial centers of Northern France, England, and the German Rhine region. Belgium's coal mines, its network of roads and canals, and the first European rail network that spread across the country by 1835 were also contributing factors. During the 19th century, Belgium was also one of the most populous countries in Europe, with a large and cheap labor pool.

Sweeping industrialization did not bypass the Belgian distilleries, either. Innovative producers installed steam generators and engines. These new inventions, paired with the distillation column developed by Jean Baptiste Cellier-Blumenthal, enabled distillers to create a continuous distillation process. Whereas the pot still is a batch still and the liquid must be sent through the system multiple times (in "batches") providing spirits with more character and flavor, column stills are noted for speed of distillation and neutrality. Belgian interest in the distillation column may have been spurred on by the fact that Cellier-Blumenthal, a Frenchman who had settled in Brussels in 1820, was friends with Belgium's first king, Leopold I, who rose to the throne on July 21, 1831 following Belgium's independence from the Netherlands in 1830.

Since the 16th century, the Southern and Northern Low Countries shared not only a mutual love for genever but a series of crucial political, social, and religious developments. In 1815, after the inauguration of Willem I as King of the Low Countries, the South (modern day Belgium) revolted against his dictatorial regime. Under his ruling, the South had been heavily underrepresented, even though they made up a larger part of the Low Countries' population and their army. The primarily Roman Catholic South demanded freedom of religion and education from the largely Protestant North. Pressure from Willem I to linguistically unify his people, including going so far as to declare Dutch the official language, also sparked unrest among the French-speaking Walloons and soldiers, as well as the French-speaking nobles in Flanders.

The Belgian Revolution, a revolt against Willem I, led to a separation of South and North, and the creation of modern day Belgium and the Netherlands in 1830. The sovereign Belgian government drastically lowered taxes on genever and banned the importation of genever from the Netherlands. The Belgian genever industry started to flourish, and in a four-year period the number of genever distilleries exploded from 599 to 1092, all in a country roughly the size of the state of Maryland.

Many of these distilleries installed the new inventions, creating efficiencies in the distillation process. As a result, the genever yield boomed, leading to a thriving export economy, underlined by the record export of 101,285 hl (2,675,666 gallons) of genever in 1872. Export data of Belgian genever to the Americas has not been found; if there was any trade, it was limited. Belgian genever would not make its official landing on American shores until the 21st century. It was my thirst for genever that led to the founding of Flemish Lion, the first importing company to bring Belgian genever to the US in 2010.

At the end of the 19th century, Belgium had enormous alcohol production facilities. The most impressive industrial distillery was the Meeus distillery in Antwerp, established in 1869 with ties to Het Anker distillery dating back to 1753. The Meeus distillery had 12 grain mills, 11 different distillation columns, its own fire brigade, and even a factory chapel. The Meeus distillery was able to produce 50,000 liters of alcohol of 50% alcohol by volume (ABV) on a daily basis. In 1884, they produced nearly 100,000 hl (2,641,720 gallons) of genever, which amounted to about a sixth of Belgium's total genever production. A portion of this distillery's genever production was exported to Spain, Brazil, Africa, Indonesia, New

Zealand, Australia, and China.

Like most Belgian distilleries, the Meeus distillery would be completely stripped of copper during World War I by occupying German forces, which they melted down for artillery shell casings. Little of the original distillery remains today, aside from the company name and parts of the old building.

*Poster Louis Meeus Distillery,*
*Wijnegem (Antwerp), Flanders, Belgium c. 1890*

*Poster Louis Meeus Distillery,*
*Wijnegem (Antwerp), Flanders, Belgium early 20th century*

In the last quarter of the 19th century, most large-scale production had moved to the cities, where factories distilled cheap, neutral alcohol from sugar beets, potatoes, and corn. After European contact with the Americas in the late 15th and early 16th centuries, explorers and traders had carried corn back to Europe and introduced it to other countries. From 1875, the Belgians started to import this cheap corn from America and, in lesser quantities, from Canada, Russia and Argentina. The Belgian government allowed the importation of this grain, with the aim of keeping the price of food low.

The massive corn importation achieved its expected result: local farmers were forced to decrease prices of their produce. Unfortunately this led to one of the biggest agricultural crises Belgium faced in the 19th century. By 1878, distillers also started to use this cheaper grain to make genever. Corn did little to enhance the flavor of the distillate, but in addition to being a much cheaper raw ingredient than the traditional rye, wheat, and barley grains, it also provided a bigger yield, making it too good a deal to pass up.

Fueled by a wartime austerity measure that limited barley consumption, cheap, neutral alcohol was used more frequently for the creation of genever, which resulted in a loss of the characteristic grain taste and the emergence of a new style of genever. Distillers who still produced genever in the old manner protested against this new method of production and stressed that their genever was prepared in accordance with the *vieux système* (French for "old method").

A distinction developed between *oude* (old) and *jonge* (young) styles of genever, delineating between traditional and more industrialized production techniques, not the age of the alcohol in the barrel. The old style is malty and sweet, containing a high proportion of malt wine distilled in an alembic. The young style is lighter and drier, with a higher proportion of neutral alcohol and a much lower proportion of malt wine.

The competition from cheap industrial alcohol, as well as artificial fertilizers dealt a serious blow to farm-based genever distillers, whose production was part of a larger cycle of grain and livestock growth. Faced with this stiff competition, many distillers cloaked themselves in the argument for quality, maintaining that genever should be produced according the *vieux système* on the basis of grain, seasonality, and tradition. Unfortunately for them, the industrial competition was too strong. Most agricultural distilleries only survived thanks to the sale of cattle and stable manure. Eventually many had to close their doors.

In 1843, there were 455 Belgian farm distilleries, but by 1900 the number had dropped to 244. Only 24 remained in 1913. Today, Stokerij Van Damme, founded in 1862 in East-Flanders, is the very last remaining farm distillery in the entire Benelux (Belgium, the Netherlands and Luxembourg). Even though the amount of farm distilleries had dropped, the country's alcohol production, driven by the industrial distilleries, only increased. By 1912, a Belgian genever production record of 835,000 hl (22,058,366 gallons) was achieved, but at the expense of traditional farm distilleries.

In the Netherlands, industrialization was slower. The industrialization gap during the 19th century between Belgium and the Netherlands was significant, and can be measured against the number of steam engines in the country: in 1837, the Netherlands counted 72 steam engines, whereas Belgium had deployed 1049 by 1839. The Dutch were also slower to adopt the distillation column, something the Belgians had already embraced in the beginning of the century.

After the Netherlands' separation from Belgium in 1830 and multiple failures to reunite, things looked grim. A stagnant economy, unfavorable weather patterns that led to crop failure after crop failure, as well as a mysterious fungus that destroyed most of the potato crops in 1845 and 1846 led to poverty, cholera, and deadly flu epidemics, slowing down Dutch progress. Despairing, thousands of Dutch sought relief outside of Europe, migrating to the Americas. It wasn't until the end of the 19th century that the Dutch managed to fully industrialize, transforming into the nation it is today. The long-awaited rise of economic and agricultural prosperity still had its pitfalls for most Dutch distilling companies. Those that never invested in the newer technologies were unable to keep up and had to face the reality of modern times.

In 1881, Schiedam was home to 392 distilleries which employed 3500 of the 5000 people in the city's labor pool. But by the end of the 19th century, those genever producers that didn't adapt as quickly to the modernization that separated the artisanal producers from the big industrial distilleries had to close their doors. The 392 distilleries dropped to 143 in ten years, and by 1920 only 14 remained. It was not until after WWII (the Dutch had remained neutral in WWI), when a grain shortage forced the distillers to reduce reliance on malt wine and use more neutral spirits, that the Dutch would fully embrace this young-style genever.

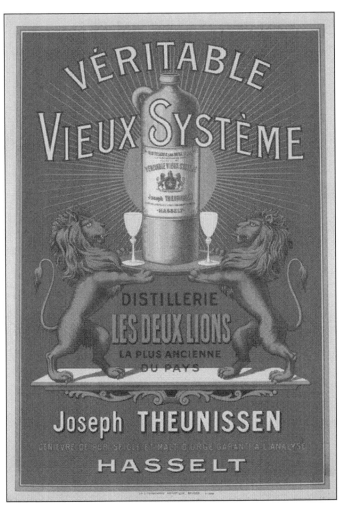

*Poster Distillery Theunissen advertising their 'Véritable Vieux Système' (French for Genuine Old Method), Hasselt, Flanders, Belgium c. 1900*

*Poster Distillery Theunissen advertising their 'Véritable Vieux Système' (French for Genuine Old Method), Hasselt, Flanders, Belgium c. 1900*

Increased production paired with a decrease in production costs led to lower prices, which allowed Belgians to incorporate significantly more genever into their daily diet. In 1850, Belgians consumed 6.5 liters of alcohol per year, rising to 9.5 liters per capita by 1899, compared to 8.2 liters for the Dutch, 4.6 liters among the British, and 3.7 liters among North Americans.

The cheaper young-style genever was primarily geared towards the poorer class, and over-indulgence led to alcoholism, further enforced poverty, and contributed to a number of other social problems. Distillers were no longer making *eau-de-vie* (French for "water of life") but *eau-de-mort* (French for "water of death"). Excessive consumption and pressure from temperance groups led to an increase in excise taxes from the authorities. The government had increased the tax on genever several times since 1835, but these efforts failed to curb the high consumption of genever, only succeeding in making the government richer.

Belgium's image abroad is one of a country full of bars and expressing a very tolerant view towards alcohol. Today, the legal age for being served alcohol in Belgium is 16 years (hence I was only a teenager when I was introduced to my first sip of genever). Public alcohol consumption is also permitted, though public intoxication is prohibited. These tolerant policies are fairly recent; during the course of the 19th century, the government declared open season on alcoholism. "Alcoholism" was a new word, coined in 1852 by Swedish doctor Magnus Huss. "Alcoholism" referred to a disease which people associated with other working class problems like prostitution, theft, slums, and begging.

**L'Alcoolisme**
D'après le tableau de Lucien Foller.
*(Appartient a l'auteur)*

*L'Alcoolisme (French for Alcoholism),*
*painting, Belgium c. 1900s*

From archived texts, the origin of the temperance movement can be traced to numerous groups concerned with public welfare, including Catholic priests, political organizations, doctors, and scholars. Printed materials from the Catholic Church prominently display a church in the background, a cross on the wall, or other traditional catholic symbols like grain and bread. To give extra power to the message, many of scenes in the print materials were shown as clear battles between right and wrong.

The twofold *Ce que donne le Blé* (French for *What grain gives*) throws this into stark contrast, setting up a positive use of grain (an ideal family spending money on bread instead of alcohol) against a negative use of grain (resulting in the distillation of alcohol and the summoning of death, represented by a skeleton looming over a family mourning their dead father).

Ce que donne le Blé

Le Pain — La Vie       L'Alcool — La Mort

*Twofold : Ce que donne le Blé (French for What grain gives)*
*Le Pain – La Vie (Bread – Life)*
*L'Acool – La Mort (Alcohol – Death)*
*Belgium c. 1900s*

This simplistic lifestyle advice was intended not only to promote healthy behavior, but to maximize productivity: a phenomenon called *'blauwe maandag'* or *'blue Monday'* arose, describing the drop in production when laborers who had consumed too much alcohol over the weekend showed up hung over or not at all. Blue Monday is a concept so deeply ingrained in Belgian culture that when my grandfather purchased his first car, he demanded one that had not been built on a Monday.

Most printed materials implied that the consumption of strong alcoholic beverages led inevitably to suffering and death. Apparently, the consumption of lighter alcoholic beverages, like wine and beer, spared people such horrible fates, as illustrated in a poster designed by painter Flori Van Acker in Bruges and published by the liberal party in Antwerp. With the slogan: *"Medeburgers uit alle standen! Onthoudt u van sterken drank!"* or *"Fellow citizens from all ranks! Withhold yourself from hard liquor!"* the entire community is called to action. The central, dominant figure is *Pietje de Dood* or Grim Reaper. Covered in a white robe with a scythe in one hand and a bottle of genever in the other, he gazes down at his victims in triumph. His victims, two dead or wasted men and a crying woman are shown in a faded black. The text across the top reads, *"Dronkenshap veroorzaakt ellende en vroegtijdige dood"* or *"Drunkenness causes misery and premature death"* points out the consequences of alcoholism.

In the last quarter of the 19th century, alcoholism became a very visible, central issue, placing other social issues on the back burner and setting the stage for the 20th century. In the Netherlands, the Dutch also went on the attack against alcohol abuse; however, genever managed to shed this negative image and would once again emerge unharmed.

*Anti-genever poster, Belgium c. 1900s*
*"Drunkenness causes misery and premature death"*

*De Nederlandsche gifboom (The Dutch poison tree)*
*Anti-alcohol drawing, the Netherlands, c. 1900*
*"Sterke Drank" - "Volks Kanker"*
*("Hard Liquor" – "Cancer of the people")*
Anti-alcohol campaigns in the Netherlands were present;
however, genever managed to shed this negative image.

# 20<sup>TH</sup> CENTURY: GENEVER'S LOSS

*Belgian genever struggles through a difficult period as genever distilleries are stripped of their copper pot stills during WWI, followed by a 1919 ban on the sale of genever in public bars that lasts until 1985. Dutch genever, escaping WWI and the ban, continues to grow in popularity.*

World War I (1914-1918) made life difficult for all of Europe, including Belgian genever producers. Even though Belgium was neutral, its strategic location on the road to France made it a prime target for Germany. Belgium had a prosperous economy leading up to the war, but four years of occupation brought the country to its knees. The Germans had mercilessly bombed cities and efficiently stripped the country bare. Machinery, spare parts, whole factories (including the roofs), had disappeared eastward.

Invading German armies stripped genever distilleries of copper stills and piping, melting down the metal for shell casings. This brought traditional genever production to a halt, almost ending a national tradition in Belgium. The Netherlands, having remained neutral through the war, were able to protect their assets from such theft.

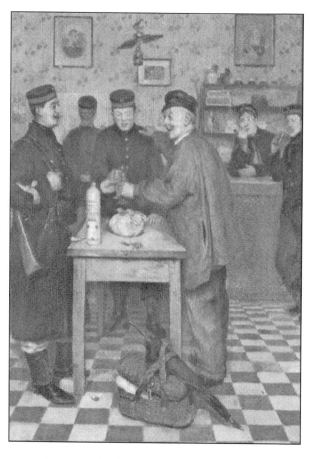

*Painting of Belgian soldiers drinking genever with the locals at a café, Belgium c. 1914*

Stokerij De Moor was founded in 1910 in Aalst, East-Flanders, and is one of the many genever distilleries that faced the cruelties of war. Its founder, Frans De Moor, lost his life in 1914 when he refused to relinquish his copper pot still to German occupiers. He was executed in full view of the public on the town's bridge across the River Dender and stabbed with a bayonet to ensure his death. After seeing Frans De Moor shot and stabbed to death, his wife, Anna, rebuilt the distillery in defiance.

Four generations later, Stokerij De Moor continues to handcraft genever from first grain to last drop, preserving the time-honored tradition of using copper pot stills, premium grains, and all-natural ingredients. Now known as Belgium's smallest active grain distillery, in 2010, Stokerij De Moor became the first distillery in history to bring Belgian genever to North-American shores. The distillery's variety of authentic genevers are imported by Flemish Lion and sold under the brand name Diep9.

*Frans De Moor (1864-1914) & Anna Lafon (1865-1930), founders of Stokerij De Moor, Aalst, East-Flanders, Belgium*

The Belgian genever industry was dealt a second blow in 1919, when the *Wet Vandervelde* or Vandervelde Law, introduced by socialist Emile Vandervelde (1866-1938), was enacted as an answer to excessive liquor consumption, prohibiting the serving of all spirits in public bars. Vandervelde was a fervent opponent of alcohol consumption, considering even one glass per day to be excessive. This radical ban came shortly before the official introduction of the shorter 8-hour work day in 1921. The Belgian government was afraid that laborers, now with more time on their hands, would visit bars en masse.

The harsh reality was that by banning alcohol in public places, alcoholism circumvented the law by moving from the bar to home. The government countered by increasing the already high taxes on genever fourfold. Combined with the fact that liquor stores sold a minimum of 2 liters of genever and set against the average earnings of Belgian workers at the time, it was only a matter of time before demand for genever collapsed.

Many bar and restaurant owners complained vociferously about a stance that put them at a severe disadvantage to neighboring countries. The Germans had schnapps, Luxembourg had kirsch, France had pastis and cognac, the British had gin, and the Dutch had genever. Belgium's elite still had easy access to liquor, but bar and restaurant patrons had to make do with beer or water.

Belgium's strong beer culture and industry owe quite a bit to this period. After competition from spirits was blunted by the temperance movement, brewers moved to fill the gap, increasing the relatively low alcohol content of beer to "console" drinkers forced to give up genever. The consumption of genever, once the most popular spirit in Belgium, had officially begun its decline, paving the way for the popularity of Belgian beer as we know it today.

On the eve of World War I, the Belgians consumed about 5.5 liters of genever per capita (a four liter decrease since 1899 driven by the temperance movement). Consumption dropped even more to 1 to 2 liters per capita in 1919. This prohibition on the serving of spirits prompted a strong reaction from the genever distillers, wholesalers and retailers. Using posters, flyers, and other channels, they pleaded for an amendment to the law.

An example of this multimedia protest is the poster from the Antwerp Hotel, Bar & Restaurant Union shown on pages 64-65. On the left side of this caricature, the bar *'Bij Pitje'* is closed, the windows are boarded up, and two officers stand guard at the door while a drunk collects his tears in his hat. However, at the grocery store *'Bij Mitje'* across the street, a long line of customers waits to legally purchase genever (a minimum of 2 liters as required by law) under the watchful eye of police officers. Even a dog walks out with a bottle of genever. A well-dressed couple in the foreground mocks the law that genever can no longer be consumed in public, but they make sure not to catch the attention of the police. The couple's rich attire serves to illustrate the fact that, under the new law, only the rich could afford the minimum volume.

The right half of the caricature shows *"De accijnzen op zoek naar alkool"* or *"The excise taxes in search of alcohol."* Customs agents are searching everywhere: under the bar, under the floor, in the wall, in the toilet, and even in the hair of the bar owner, while a couple in the background drinks out of large glasses. This also serves to mock the law and how patrons got around it by drinking genever by ordering a *"Spa Maison."* "Spa" is a Belgian mineral water, so *"Spa Maison"* means "water of the house." To mislead the customs agents, genever was served in a water glass. This poster may have hung in a public place such as a hotel or bar, and the establishment owner scratched out *"De accijnzen"* or *"The excise taxes"* to prevent complaints from government patrons.

It was not until 1985 (yes, 1985!) that the ban on sales of spirits in bars was lifted, although most people had stopped obeying the law by the seventies. This lift of the Vandervelde Law after 66 years ultimately had nothing to do with giving in to popular demand, and everything to do with tax revenue. It was common knowledge that, despite the ban, public places were still serving genever, and underground distilleries and smuggling rings were lucrative occupations. *"I smell the alcohol from 200 meters away"* or *"He was hidden in his kettle"* are only some of the statements made by the former customs detectives.

The smuggling of genever had been common for centuries in Belgium as well as the Netherlands, but smuggling in Flanders really gained momentum after the independence of Belgium from the Netherlands in 1830. At that time a vast difference in tax policies between both countries fueled the already active alcohol smuggling and underground distilling. While the Dutch and the Belgians had smuggling in their blood, large-scale illegal distilleries only existed on the Flemish side of the border, particularly in the countryside in the regions of Antwerp. Remarkably, during the years between wars, war widows were the primary culprits, running illicit distilleries to support their families.

The genever culture in the Netherlands never missed a beat; being spared the Vandervelde law, the Dutch were able to keep the genever flowing in bars. The impact of the Vandervelde Law can still be felt today in the common misconception that genever is a Dutch creation, that the Belgians are beer-drinkers with no claim to genever.

Unfortunately, most people have forgotten Belgium's crucial role in the invention, production, and consumption of genever. It hasn't helped that pre-1830 *België* (Belgium) and *Nederland* (the Netherlands), were collectively called *De Nederlanden* (The Low Countries), and both populations mostly speak Dutch. From descriptions like 'a Dutch manuscript' or 'a Dutch movie', you are unable to determine whether it was produced by the Dutch or the Flemish. The same can be said of an English manuscript or an English movie, which can be of American or British origin. Only those familiar with the Dutch language are able to differentiate dialects and countries of origin. When I speak Dutch, the Dutch will immediately hear that I'm from Belgium, and the Flemish will even be able to pinpoint which city I'm from, since the Flemish dialect I speak is only regional to Ghent. The Dutch pronunciation of genever varies too. Genever in Flanders is pronounced as [juh-nay-ver], with a more pronounced French 'g', whereas in the Netherlands it is pronounced as [jeh-nay-ver] with a soft 'j'.

Throughout history, the various Dutch dialects have gotten jumbled together, further contributing to the misattribution of genever's origin. But this is all about to change.

64

*Poster Locomotief Genever*
*Schiedam, Holland, the Netherlands c. 1950*
*'Met "Locomotief" steeds fit en actief!'*
*(With "Locomotief" always fit and active!)*
While the Belgians could no longer serve genever in bars,
the Dutch were still allowed to pour genever and
promote its health benefits.

# 21ˢᵀ CENTURY:
# GENEVER'S RENAISSANCE

*Traditional genever production is now on the rise. Fueled by national pride, recognition across Europe, and a renewed passion for regional products, genever enjoys a revival.*

Belgium and the Netherlands have entire bars, celebrations, museums, and TV-shows devoted to their national and historic spirit. With the lift of the *Wet Vandervelde* on January 1, 1985, genever bars in Belgium could open up again.

In 1985, De Vagant in the medieval streets of Antwerp, and in 1986, 't Dreupelkot in the medieval streets of Ghent opened its doors, as well. Both now offer more than 200 different Belgian genevers and entertain visitors from around the world. Many more Belgian genever bars opened their doors in the years that followed. At 't Spul, a genever bar in Schiedam, you can taste more than 400 different Dutch and Belgian genevers. The owner, Rob van Klaarwater, is so passionate about the history of his national spirit that he even created his own museum in a building adjacent to the bar showcasing his impressive personal collection of preserved genever bottles, glassware, posters and historical information alike.

*De Vagant, a genever bar in Antwerp, Flanders, Belgium*

*'t Spul, a genever bar in Schiedam, Holland, the Netherlands*

In 1987, in the middle of Hasselt in a 19th century agricultural distillery, the *Nationaal Jenever Musuem* (National Genever Museum) opened, telling the fascinating history of Belgian genever. Visitors are invited to follow the genever production process and sample a wide variety of Belgian genevers, including several genevers distilled once a year for ten weeks at the stokerij of this museum according to centuries-old traditions. Nine years later, the *Nationaal Jenever Museum* (National Genever Museum), in Schiedam opened its doors. In the stokerij of this genever museum, they still craft malt wine using a recipe from 1700.

*The National Genever Museum, Hasselt, Flanders, Belgium*

Every year, Hasselt throws an enormous genever festival known as the *jeneverfeesten*. For two days, the festival celebrates genever in every color and flavor paired with music, street theatre, parades, and culinary genever attractions. During this two-day festival, the water flowing from a bronze fountain in the market center, gifted by the city in 1981 as a reminder of Hasselt's rich genever tradition, is replaced with genever! In 2011, Belgium added another yearly festival to celebrate its national spirit: *O'de Flander Oost-Vlaamse Jenever Feesten*, a two-day genever festival in Ghent, celebrating East-Flemish genevers. In 2013, Amsterdam started hosting a yearly, two-day genever festival including a 'Mixing & Cocktails with Genever' contest, formerly hosted in Schiedam.

*Jenever Festival (Genever Festival) logo on barrels, Amsterdam, Holland, the Netherlands*

In 2008, a 10-part Belgian-made TV-show *"De Smaak van De Keyser"* (The Taste of De Keyser) started airing on Belgian, Dutch, and French TV. This award-winning family drama tells the story of three generations of women in a Hasselt distillery. It's the story of an exciting and mysterious search for truth and the ultimate taste of genever. A must see!

Recognized for its historic and cultural contribution to Europe, genever received a special European Union seal of *appellation d'origine contrôlée* or *AOC* on January 15, 2008. Translated to "controlled designation of origin" or "terroir", this is meant as a protection for specific foods and spirits produced in Europe. It was also bestowed on Cognac and Scottish whisky.

Terroirs are indicating factors attributed to specific locations, including the soil, topography, and climate. These terroir characteristics get transferred to the genever through the distillation process, affecting the taste of the final distillate. The *Protected Designation of Origin* or *Protected Geographical Indication* ensures that only genever distilled in traditional regions of Europe – namely Belgium and the Netherlands, along with specific regions of France and Germany – may bear the name *genever/jenever/genièvre*.

The document dictating the details is *Regulation (EC) No. 110/2008 of the European Parliament and of the Council of 15 January 2008* on the definition, description, presentation, labeling, and the protection of geographical origins of spirit drinks, includes the following terroirs, of which most are exclusive to Belgium: *genever* (exclusive to Belgium, the Netherlands, and small regions in France and Germany), *grain genever* (exclusive to Belgium, the Netherlands, and small regions in France), *old genever* (exclusive to Belgium and the Netherlands), *young genever* (exclusive to Belgium and the Netherlands), *fruit genever* (exclusive to Belgium, the Netherlands, and small regions in France and Germany), *O'de Flander East-Flemish grain genever* (exclusive to Belgium), *Hasselt genever* (exclusive to Belgium),

*Balegem genever* (exclusive to Belgium), *Peket* (exclusive to Belgium), *Flanders Artois genever* (exclusive to France) and *East-Frisia cereal/grain genever* (exclusive to Germany).

Today, Americans still refer to genever as gin, Dutch gin or Holland gin. Side-by-side comparison reveals these as inaccurate identifications. The terms "gin" and "genever" refer to different things. Gin derives its predominant flavor from the juniper berries that are added to a neutral spirit. Lining up different gins, the differences among them are largely assessed by their botanical profiles. Botanicals are also important to genever, but it derives its predominant flavor by pot-distilling a fermented grain mash (malt wine), so the discussion centers around the malty grain taste. The production process and characteristics of gin and genever, while sharing much common ground, are still quite different, and correct identification is essential. I like to say that "I'm a believer in genever," a helpful phrase for reminding people that genever is a distinct spirit category with unique flavors, terroirs and history. This expression also helps with the correct pronunciation of genever [juh-nee-ver], which has proven historically tricky for English speakers.

The following are the eleven genever terroirs promoting and protecting the many names and types of this unique spirit category:

# GENEVER

*Genièvre/Jenever/Genever*
This terroir is reserved for Belgium,
the Netherlands, France (Départements Nord (59)
and Pas-de-Calais (62)) and Germany (German
Bundesländer Nordrhein-Westfalen and
Niedersachsen)

Genever is a juniper-flavored spirit produced by flavoring ethyl alcohol of agricultural origin and/or grain spirit and/or grain distillate with juniper berries. Unlike gin, it does not have to have an apparent aroma or taste to it. The minimum alcoholic strength of genever has to be 30 % ABV (60 proof). The genever terroir guarantees a spirit produced in Belgium, the Netherlands, small parts of France and small parts of Germany.

The preparation of genever involves the blending of neutral alcohol and malt wine, whereas gin doesn't contain any malt wine at all. This malt wine has a very recognizable smell similar to wheat bread. The malt wine mash, closely resembling a grain mash made for whiskey, can consist of a grain mixture including any of the following: malted barley, wheat, rye, or corn. To obtain malted barley, the barley grains are cleaned, steeped in water and left to germinate first.

The obtained green malt is dried, generating a great deal of aromatic components contributing to the future taste and smell of genever. The malted barley and remaining grain mixture are ground in a mill, and poured in a heated mash tun filled with the necessary quantity of water. During mashing, the saccharification of the starch occurs where the enzymes of the malt disintegrate the starch to sugars. Yeast is added to the cooled grain mash for the fermentation to begin, converting sugars into alcohol and carbon dioxide.

After mashing and fermentation, the grain mash is distilled for the first time. Alcohol has a lower boiling point than water (78.3°C vs 100°C or 173°F vs 212°F) allowing the alcohol in the grain mash to evaporate quicker than water. When the steam (the vapors or spirits), packed with alcohol, comes in connection with a cold surface, it condenses and changes into a fluid with a higher alcohol content than the original source. By repeating this process, the alcohol content continues to increase.

The alcohol content is increased first in the *ruwnat* to about 15% ABV or 30 proof (the residue remaining after this first distillation is called draff which is served as nutritious feed for cattle and pigs), then in the *enkelnat* to about 25% ABV or 50 proof, and finally in the *bestnat* to more than 45% ABV or 90 proof. This triple distillation flows towards a measuring vat where the excise clerk determines the strength and volume (and taxes!) of the alcohol.

After measurement this unrefined alcohol is pumped into the alembic and redistilled to become malt wine. Parts of the resulting distillate (the *kop* or head and *staart* or tail) are discarded due to a relatively high level of impurities, obtaining malt spirits with an alcohol content of about 70% ABV or 140 proof. The impreciseness of the pot still distillation brings with it a rich taste and aroma to the now refined alcohol.

Once the malt wine is obtained, depending on the distiller's preference, part of it is distilled again with botanicals, resulting in an herbal-flavored malt spirit. Another part is redistilled as it is (i.e. with no botanicals). The two richly scented and tasting malt wine distillates are then recombined, filtered, and blended with neutral spirit from grain or molasses, and diluted with water to the distillers' alcoholic strength of choice of the final spirit: genever. When the malt wine wasn't previously redistilled with botanicals, distillers can choose to add flavoring to the final spirit instead. The ratio of malt wine to neutral spirit determines, amongst other things, what type of genever the end product will be.

Malt wine preparation techniques have barely changed since the late 16th century and can only be made in a *branderij* (there exists no English translation of this word but can be loosely translated as a place where you burn). The remaining process takes place in a *distilleerderij* (distillery). A *stokerij* is a combination of a *branderij* and a *distilleerderij*. Today, almost all Dutch genevers are made with malt wine produced at a *stokerij* in Belgium simply because the Netherlands has almost no *branderijen* (plural of *branderij*) of their own, while in Belgium these are still spread across the country.

In a *distilleerderij*, each variety is further personalized with the addition of a wide selection of herbs that can drastically alter its composition and character, varying by region. For example, Hasselt and Holland use juniper berries with a variety of other regional and imported herbs, whereas in East-Flanders the pure grain taste commonly comes from the centuries-old malt wine recipe. About 30 different herbs can be used, including coriander, blessed thistle, Angelica root (Holy Ghost root), St. John's bread (carob), anise, and orange peel. The ingredients give the different types of genever its specific taste, smell, and color. Every distiller has their own recipe, securely locked in a safe or passed on by word through generations.

Before being blended with neutral spirits to become genever, some malt wine undergoes a long ripening process, favorably impacting its flavor, in particular when the ripening process takes place in oak barrels. Sometimes the barrels are charred before they are filled to obtain a smoky color and taste. The origin of the oak, the age of the barrels, and the length of time in the barrels all have a significant impact on flavor. Small amounts of air are allowed in the barrel through the pores of the wood so the distillate can properly develop. The exchange between barrel and its environment is constantly evaporating small amounts of the distillate. This is often called *la part des anges*, French for the angels' share. In earlier centuries, barrels weren't used to refine the taste of genever. These were just handy containers. But through experimental tasting, it was discovered that these barrels had an influence on the taste of the genever, too.

The ripening process of malt wine in barrels can take years. But don't expect to see the same color of an aged whisky, since only the malt wine, and not the entire distillate has been aged, which is why it's not called aged genever but *belegen* or *gelagerde jenever* meaning matured genever. Common in Belgium and the Netherlands are 2 to 5 year matured genevers. Harder to find are 8, 12, or 20 year matured genevers.

# GRAIN GENEVER

*Genièvre de grains, Graanjenever, Graangenever*
This terroir is reserved for Belgium,
the Netherlands and France (Départements
Nord (59) and Pas-de-Calais (62))

When *graanjenever* is mentioned on the label, you are guaranteed that only alcohol from 100% grain is used as the basis. The grains can consist of barley, rye, wheat and corn. Premium genever brands generally produce purely grain genevers and when they do, they usually don't use the cheaper, less flavorful corn in their grain mixture, sticking to the traditional rye, wheat, and barley grains.

*Rye, wheat and barley grains, the traditional raw ingredients of grain genever*

## OLD GENEVER

*Oude jenever, Oude genever*
This terroir is reserved for Belgium
and the Netherlands

*Oude* (Dutch for "old") does not refer to a matter of aging, but the distilling technique. The name old, or *vieux-système*, came into use to distinguish it from the more modern or "young-style" genever that arrived on the market in the 19th century.

Old genever has a traditional character defined by malt wine, which must contain at least 15% malt wine and can contain no more than 20 grams of sugar per liter. The result is a malty, sweet, rich spirit, typically with an oily texture. Quality old genevers usually contain anywhere from 40 to 50% malt wine, and genever containing 51% or more malt wine is no longer called *oude genever* but *korenwijn* (cereal/grain wine).

In Belgium, the minimum alcohol content for old genever is set at 30% ABV (60 proof), while the Netherlands requires old genever to have a minimum of 35% ABV (70 proof). The minimum alcohol content for *korenwijn* is 38% ABV (76% proof).

Old genever doesn't have to be matured but if it is, the malt wine has to be aged for a minimum of one year. Generally, caramel is added to give the old genever a golden color and a sweeter flavor. Instead of caramel, some artisanal distilleries rely on barrel-aging the malt wine to achieve the golden color whereas other distilleries use a combination of caramel coloring and malt wine aging.

An old genever distilled from 100% grain is called *oude graanjenever* or old grain genever. An old genever where the malt wine has been aged is called *belegen oude (graan)jenever*, *belagerde oude (graan)jenever* or matured old (grain) genever with the amount of years it matured at the beginning or the back of the description. For example *2 jaar belegen oude (graan)jenever* (quite a mouth full), so it's common to drop the word *'belegen'* and just call it a *2 jaar oude (graan)jenever* (2 year old (grain) genever).

*Old Genever label, origin and date unknown. Vieux Genievre – Pur Grain – Oude Graan Genever (Old genever- Pure Grain – Old Grain Genever)*

## YOUNG GENEVER

*Jonge jenever, jonge genever*
This terroir is reserved for Belgium
and the Netherlands

As with old genever, *jonge* (Dutch for "young") does not refer to the aging period, but to distilling techniques. A worldwide trend toward a lighter and less dominant taste, driven by innovations in distilling techniques during the 19th century and grain shortages during the World Wars, led to the development of young genever.

By law, young genever can contain no more than 15% malt wine and no more than 10 grams of sugar per liter. This colorless genever, known for its neutral taste, is now the most popular style of genever. This style is closest to the familiar London Dry gin, though the maltiness and light use of botanicals sets it apart.

In Belgium, the minimum alcohol content for young genever is set at 30% ABV (60 proof), while the Netherlands requires young genever to have a minimum of 35% ABV (70 proof).

A young genever distilled from 100% grain is called *jonge graanjenever* or young grain genever. It is rare, but there exist young genevers where the malt wine has been aged, creating *belegen jonge (graan)jenever, belagerde jonge (graan)jenever* or matured young (grain) genever.

# FRUIT GENEVER

*Genièvre aux fruits/Vruchtenjenever/*
*Jenever met vruchten/Fruchtgenever*
This terroir is reserved for Belgium,
the Netherlands, France (Départements Nord(59)
and Pas-de-Calais (62)) and Germany (German
Bundesländer Nordrhein-Westfalen and
Niedersachsen)

Unlike genever, fruit genever is not categorized by the European Union as a 'juniper-flavored spirit' but as 'other spirit drinks.' The alcohol content of fruit genever is between 18 and 24% ABV (36 and 48 proof).

In the 1980s, it became popular in Flanders to macerate the young genever with fresh fruit. The fruit genevers allowed the distillers to attract a younger audience, and those who, due to the Vandervelde ban from 1919 until 1985, were not used to drinking higher alcohol beverages in bars.

Fruit genever comes in different flavors like red currant, passion fruit, apple, lemon, kiwi, and cherry, to name a few of the dozens available flavors in Belgium. Unlike flavored vodkas, which are still colorless, fruit genevers are packed with all-natural fruit juice and pulp, imparting the natural colors and fresh taste of its fruit. It should be noted that there are some artificially flavored and colored fruit genevers out there too.

My favorite fruit flavor coincides with Belgium's

most traditional, popular, and delightfully tart fruit: *aalbes* or red currant. Due to its popularity, this berry, originally from Belgium, Germany, France, the Netherlands, Northern Italy, and Northern Spain, is simply called *bes* (berry). When macerated into *jonge jenever* this *fruit jenever* is simply called *bessenjenever* (berry genever).

*Ribes Rubrum, drawing of a red currant bush and red currants*

In Belgium, fruit genever has a passionate following, and is now outselling young and old genever, whereas in the Netherlands fruit genevers are still gaining traction, and young genever remains by far the most popular.

In the past decade, a new trend in Belgium has emerged, adding cream to the young genever with popular flavors like chocolate, vanilla, and *speculoos* (a traditional Belgian biscuit). This was followed by a traditional Belgian candy-infused genever: *neuzeke* or *cuberdon*. Recently, even a Belgian waffle-flavored genever has debuted on the market.

## HASSELT GENEVER

*Hasseltse jenever*
This terroir is exclusive to Belgium
(Hasselt, Zonhoven, Diepenbeek)

The *Hasseltse jenever* terroir guarantees an authentic and quality genever crafted in Hasselt, Flanders, Belgium. The minimum alcohol content for Hasselt genever is 30% ABV or 60 proof.

Hasselt genever, more than any other Belgian genevers, imparts the taste of juniper berries and a variety of other exotic herbs. Hasselt was saved from the distilling ban and distiller migration during the 17th century. Benefiting from a steady supply of grain, genever production soared, and the reputation holds true even today: Hasselt is the genever capital of Belgium, home of the National Genever Museum, and host of Belgium's yearly genever festival.

Schiedam, the genever capital of the Netherlands, was not given a specific terroir but the city awards some of their locally produced genevers with a domestic *Schiedamse Garantiezegel* (Schiedam Guarantee Seal) guaranteeing customers an authentic, quality genever crafted in Schiedam.

# O'DE FLANDER
# EAST-FLEMISH GRAIN GENEVER

*O' de Flander-Oost-Vlaamse graanjenever*
This terroir is exclusive to Belgium
(Oost-Vlaanderen)

The *O'de Flander-Oost-Vlaamse graanjenever* or simply *O'de Flander* terroir guarantees an authentic, quality grain genever crafted entirely in East-Flanders, Belgium. The minimum alcohol content for an O'de Flander young or old genever is 35% ABV or 70 proof. O'de Flander genever typically imparts the pure grain taste coming from the centuries-old malt wine recipe.

Around 1883, a quarter of the industrial distilleries and two thirds of the agricultural distilleries were based in East-Flanders. Today there are only about fifteen genever-producing distilleries in East-Flanders, ten of which still craft genuine East-Flemish grain genever.

*O'de Flander seal guaranteeing a genuine grain genever crafted in East-Flanders, Belgium*

# BALEGEM GENEVER

*Balegemse jenever*
This terroir is exclusive to Belgium
(Balegem)

The *Balegemse jenever* terroir certifies an authentic, quality grain genever crafted in Balegem, a town in East-Flanders, Belgium. It is home to Stokerij Van Damme, founded in 1862, the very last farm distillery in the Benelux (Belgium, the Netherlands, and Luxembourg). During summer on the farm, they grow the grains needed to craft genever, the genever itself is made from December through April, and the manure from the cattle is used on the land to grow the crops. The farm distillery also has guestrooms for aficionados to visit and soak up the tradition.

## PEKET

*Peket/pékèt (de Wallonie)*
This terroir is exclusive to Belgium
(Wallonia)

When *Peket* is mentioned on the label, you are guaranteed a genever crafted in Wallonia, the southern, French-speaking part of Belgium (see page 22 for a map). The word Peket means *piquant* (spicy) in the old Walloon language (a French dialect) referring to the spicy taste from the juniper berries present in genever crafted in Wallonia.

## FLANDERS ARTOIS GENEVER

*Genièvre Flandres Artois*
This terroir is exclusive to France
(Départements Nord (59) and Pas-de-Calais (62))

When *Genièvre Flandres Artois* is displayed on the
label, you are guaranteed a genever crafted in Flanders
Artois, French Flanders, France (see page 22 for a
map). During the 17th century, Flanders Artois was
annexed from the Southern Low Countries by the
French and is still coinciding today with the current
Belgian-French border.

## EAST FRISIA
## CEREAL GRAIN GENEVER

*Ostfriesischer Korngenever*
This terroir is exclusive to Germany
(Ostfriesland)

When *Ostfriesischer Korngenever* is displayed on the label, you are guaranteed a genever crafted from 100% cereal grain in Ostfriesland (East-Frisia or Eastern Friesland). Formerly part of the Low Countries, this coastal region is located in the northwest of the German federal state of Niedersachsen along the Dutch-German border (see page 22 for a map).

# THE GENEVER
# BOTTLE

Until the beginning of the 19th century, distilleries used barrels and large jugs to provide genever to the local market. With the growing trade and export of genever, distillers began to think in ever more commercial ways.

A spirit full of history and character as genever deserves a suitable package. At first they used expensive glass *kelderflessen*, or cellar bottles, before switching to earthenware jugs. Unlike barrels, these sturdy jugs do not alter the taste of genever, are impervious to light, provide an excellent protection against temperature fluctuations, and are easy to unload off the boat and get into the trade. Genever was bottled and shipped around the world in these handcrafted brown or beige clay bottles, which can still be found in old shipwrecks. These historic bottles can also be found at antique shops, including the one down the street from my house in Richmond, Vermont.

The clay bottle's iconic shape is recognizable and

unique to genever. From the second half of the 19th century most jugs were trademarked, receiving a stamp with the name of the distillery. This handcrafted clay genever bottle is called *jeneverstoop* (genever jug), simply *stoop* (jug), or *kruik* (jug).

*Poster of Netherlands Distilleries, Holland, the Netherlands c. 1920, showcasing the kelderfles (cellar bottle)*

*Traditional genever jugs, Belgium c. 1890-1935*
View this picture in color on the cover of this book.

Throughout history, many individual professions were associated with the larger genever industry, some of which have all but vanished. Among them is the *kruikenruiker* or jug smeller. For this profession you needed a special attribute: a good nose. Previously, distilleries had to pay taxes on genever jugs and bottles; during World War I (1914-1918), the taxes on a bottle doubled, driven by the lack of raw materials. This led to distilleries collecting and reusing the genever jugs in order to avoid the bottle tax. Prior to being refilled, returned bottles had to be cleaned thoroughly, which was not an easy task with the opaque jugs.

Many distillers hired a special jug smeller, a specialist who, with their nose, could determine what had been in the bottle. The jug smeller had to obey strict rules, prohibited from smoking or eating spicy foods that might interfere with the task, if they wanted to be able to sniff with each nostril if in one bottle there had been petroleum, vegetable oil, or cigarette butts.

Increasing post-World-War prosperity brought about a change in drinking habits. The bar stool in the local café was no longer the only favorite spot for a drink: lounging in an easy chair at home in front of the radio or TV, with a drink at hand, became an increasingly attractive alternative. The demand for genever drawn straight from the barrel declined rapidly and those who fancied a drink now tended to ask for a bottle of a specific brand. Distillers responded to the new trend by bottling all their genevers, not only for export but for local consumption, too. Customers were able to recognize their regular genever brand by the iconic shape of the bottle and the colorful labels bearing the registered trade name. This was the height of the genever jug's popularity.

In 1945, after the Second World War, many distilleries switched from these traditional clay jugs back to the now cheaper glass bottles. Glass had been produced in the Low Countries for over 3,000 years, but until the advent of mechanical glass production, glass bottles were a luxury product and therefore very expensive. Today, most genever is packaged in green or clear glass bottles, and there are very few manufacturers left producing handcrafted clay genever bottles. Many jug manufacturers switched to machine based manufacturing to compete with the cheaper glass alternatives.

I visited an 8th generation "Jug Baker," where every iconic genever bottle is made by hand. The family company was founded in 1800 to produce jugs for mineral water, and these water jugs were the first jugs the distillers used as an alternative to the *kelderfles* (cellar bottle). This same company is now one of the last producers of handcrafted clay genever bottles, also producing all the clay bottles for Diep9, the first Belgian genever imported to the US.

The "Jug Baker" is based along the clay-dominated banks of the Rhine in Koblenz, Germany, the ideal location for the sourcing of its raw material, clay, and the shipping of its handmade products. The clay arrives in the clay cellar before undergoing a mixing process with water to prepare a lump of clay for the beginning of a new piece. The clay lumps are placed into a jug machine, where the jug baker strives to create a unique but uniform, one-of-a-kind product. This is where each bottle receives its beautiful little imperfections, which can clearly be seen around the neck of the bottle. Once the clay bottle's iconic profile is shaped and has dried, a glaze is applied to the genever bottles. Now the stoneware is ready for the kiln process, and is placed in an oven with a firing temperature of 1240 °C or 2264 °F for a couple of hours. After undergoing critical testing, the bottles are shipped to distilleries in Belgium and the Netherlands, where they are filled with these countries' national spirit and sealed with a cork before being enjoyed by craft spirit enthusiasts around the world.

When you come across a handcrafted clay genever bottle, check out its imperfections, as every bottle is unique. Having seen the clay bottle's labor intensive production process firsthand, I never throw away an empty piece of art. Even though their disposal is still extremely environmentally friendly, I reuse the bottles for olive oil containers, flower vases, candle holders, and art projects.

Fortunately, the historic genever jug is gaining popularity again with the renewed interest in presentation and packaging of genever. The earthenware bottle symbolizes the preservation of traditional distilling techniques and recipes. Many spirit brands spend a lot of money on design firms to come up with a bottle shape unique to its brand, but traditional genever distilleries are proud to choose heritage over fashionable bottle design trends.

## GENEVER
## DRINKING RITUALS

Before the 16th century, bars did not exist as we think of them today. There were hostels, taverns, and lodging houses focused on providing food, rest, and shelter to travelers. During the 17th century, coffee became popular in Europe. The availability and popularity of coffee resulted in the creation of *koffiehuizen* (coffee houses), eventually simplified to cafés. The word café comes from the French word for coffee. In time, the meaning of the word café changed, from a location where primarily coffee was drunk to a place where primarily alcoholic beverages are consumed. This same change in meaning can be observed in the use of the term *koffieshop*, primarily used in Amsterdam to denote a place to buy cannabis, as well as coffee.

Cafés fulfilled an important social function where local politics were discussed while people enjoyed a drink. They were the centers of the business as well as the political and social life of the city. It is not unusual to make a stop at the café on the way home from work. In the days when a paycheck was still paid in hard cash instead of direct deposit, patronage would have been predictably high at the end of the week. Some employers even paid their laborers at the local café, resulting in major money mismanagement! Current laws now prohibit employers from paying their employees in bars and restaurants (bar and restaurant owners excluded).

Cafés also go by the name *bruin café* or brown café (referring to the dark and cozy wood decoration), *kroeg* or *stamcafé* (literally translated as tribe bar, a place where you know everybody's name and where the waiter, upon entering, already prepares your drink without any questions asked, making you feel at home). Cafés which were originally or still are attached to a genever distillery to provide samples of their wares to potential buyers are called *proeflokalen* (tasting rooms).

Genever formed a source of inspiration to artists, and cafés were a favorite subject for paintings in the 19th century. Paintings from those times offer us keen insights into scenes from the daily life of the cafés, depicting life as simple and predictable but often hard and lonely, with genever as a drink that united the rich, the poor, and the overindulgent.

*Scenes from the daily life in Belgian cafés c. 1900*

The Belgians and the Dutch often enjoy genever neat and ice cold, but connoisseurs tend to savor it at room temperature. The older and more authentic a genever is, the less it is recommended to be consumed too cold for the sake of taste and aroma. Genever has been around for centuries, long before the refrigerator was invented. Back then, a bottle of genever (old genever) was just sitting on the shelf of a cabinet and not the shelf of a freezer. On the flip side, young genever and fruit genever with a less subtle character are often considered to taste better at lower temperatures, and thus kept in the refrigerator or freezer.

Little is known of the original genever drinking vessels which is in stark contrast to wine and beer glasses that were in documented use prior to 1600. Because of genever's high alcohol content, we can guess that it was drunk from relatively small glasses. During the 17th century, there was no standard genever glass but based on paintings, cards, and archeological sites from the era, people drank from a broad range of small drinking vessels.

It wasn't until the 18th century that the modern genever glass began to take form as an hour-glass-shaped and shot-glass-sized drinking vessel with a wide mouth and a stem. Toward the middle of the 18th century, a new type of glass arrived on the scene: a small hour-glass-shaped glass with a short stem and a heavy, flat foot. Its narrow body, wide mouth, and solid glass base allowed for easy holding and drinking. Today, this type of shot glass is the preferred genever drinking vessel in Belgium, whereas the long-stemmed hour-glass or tulip-shaped version is preferred in the Netherlands. Most bars feature their personalized genever glasses, making these shot glasses an enjoyable collector's item. But the optimal genever glassware is a tulip-shaped cognac glass that has a long stem and a bell that opens up towards to top, slightly flaring outwards. The shape allows the nose to be concentrated towards the top, making the genever tasting experience even more special.

*From left to right:*
1. *My grandmother's genever shot glass with a flat foot and silver plated holder.*
2. *Traditional Dutch genever tulip shot glass.*
3. *Tulip-shaped cognac glass filled with old genever.*

The national spirit, served in its genever shot glass of choice, is sipped and savored not downed as a shot, which first comes to mind when a shot glass is involved. Traditionally, genever is poured to the brim of shot glasses, and since modern times, the glassware is taken directly from the freezer.

The first step to drinking genever properly is to keep the glass on the table, bend down to the glass and take the first sip without holding the glass. Once this traditional first sip is taken, one can enjoy the rest of the drink normally. The story goes that this drinking tradition stems from back in the day when workers did not have a lot of money to spend on personal pleasures. Drinking genever with friends at the local café was their primary outlet. With the little discretionary income they had to spend, they wanted to get their money's worth, demanding to have their glasses filled to the brim. Instead of lifting the glass, risking spilling a drop, the first sip was taken without any hands. Depending on current bar traditions and policy, if the last pour from a bottle is not enough to fill the shot glass, the customer receives the drink for free.

Common in Flanders is the *duikboot* ("submarine") where a shot of genever, fruit genever in particular, is poured in a beer. Another drinking ritual, more common in the Netherlands, is a *kopstootje* ("little head butt") where a shot of genever is paired with a beer. The *kopstootje* is started with the traditional genever sip from the shot glass followed by a sip of beer, and so on. Both young and old genever can be paired with a beer of choice, preferably a Pale Ale or Lager and fruit genever pairs well with a white Belgian beer.

*Poster Henkes Genever, Holland, the Netherlands c. 1960*
The first step to drinking genever properly is to keep the glass
on the table, bend down to the glass and take the first sip
without holding the glass.

When the Flemish and the Dutch order a shot of genever they ask for a *druppel, dreupel,* or *borrel* meaning drop or dram, the medieval word for little drink. Other popular genever synonyms are: an *oude klare* or *jonge klare* (a clear old or young genever without the addition of bitters and sugar), a *witteke* (in some parts of Flanders it refers to genever, in other parts it refers to a white beer) or a *jonkie* (referring to a young genever, most popular in Holland).

The Dutch language has a wide array of terms to describe drinking, alcohol, and drunkenness. There's even a book by Ewoud Sanders, *Borrel Woordenboek 750 namen voor onzen glazen boterham,* containing 750 different words from the Netherlands and Flanders for *"borrel"* and *"jenever,"* a stunning collection from the 16th century to today.

In the past it was believed that a *borrel* was good for your health. Those who needed an excuse to sip a shot glass filled to the brim with genever, were able to cite its many written medicinal properties. An example of this is Robert Hennebo (1685-1737), a Dutchman dubbed the *jeneverdichter* (genever poet) writing in rhyme that genever in the morning freshens up people and makes them healthy and genever in the afternoon repairs the stomach and liver:

*Jenever in den Morgenstond,*
*Verfrist, en maakt den Mensch gezond.*
*Wanneer de Zuyer Zon om hoog,*
*Maakt Magen swak, en leevers droog,*
*Dan ziet men hoe door de Jenever*
*De Maag hersteld word, en de Leever.*

The unconcerned way Hennebo touted genever indicates how casually accepted alcohol consumption was in the beginning of the 18th century. Nowadays, not a single distiller would consider marketing genever consumption from morning till night, day in day out. Even so, a belief in the magical healing power of genever persists in many places, such as my house, commonly enjoying a *borrel* a day, more appropriate of today's time, a tradition passed on to me by my grandmother.

Lots of modern scientific research concerning genever's health benefits has been done, but, as we see with studies on the health effects of wine, the conclusions change based on the researcher or the outlet reporting them, so I can't give you a concrete scientific answer. Today, distillers can't make any health claims on their libations, but the tradition of wishing each other *gezondheid* (to your health) when drinking genever is still in practice in Belgium and the Netherlands. The more common and trendy word for *gezondheid* in Belgium is *santé* whereas in the Netherlands it is *proost*.

When you drink a couple of *borrels* (plural for *borrel*) with friends at your *stamcafé,* and feel the need to sing (of which I too am often guilty), there are plenty of songs to express your fondness of this historic spirit. De Stoopkes (literally meaning the little jugs, referring to the traditional clay genever bottles), a musical entertainment group founded in Hasselt in 1985 (the same year when genever could start flowing in Belgian bars again!), sing about life with and without alcohol, in particular life with and without genever.

*Ons Jeneverke* (Our Little Genever), is a drinking

song about how hard life and work can be, begging to allow us to keep our genever, a nod to the 20th century ban on genever the Belgians had to endure for so long. Here's my best attempt on translating the nuances of this song, originally written in a Flemish dialect:

*Our Little Genever*

*You know people, life is no joke,*
*Work every day, yes, what did you think*
*Taxes and invoices fall into your mailbox*
*Tickets, forms, no, they don't give you any rest*
*That's why we take a moment of blissful happiness*
*And hang this annoying world on a yoke*
*Give Jesus his share, give the king his part*
*But leave us our little genever*

*Going to work every day, we stay well-behaved*
*But leave us our little genever*
*It makes me want to sing*
*It's in my blood*
*It makes me want to jump*
*I don't know how to contain myself*
*So give Jesus his share, give the king his part*
*But leave us our little genever*

*But you know, people, life isn't a joke,*
*Dieting every day, yes what did you think*
*Because everybody has to be skinnier and more fit*
*Everybody has to be prettier than its own mirror*
*That's why we take that moment and put us to show*
*In our Lord his mirror we are all the same*

*TV, computer, skiing, everything has its time*
*But our Hasselt genever*
*I don't want to lose anymore*
*for any money in the world*

*Poster Distillery Bekaert, St. Amandsberg,*
*Ghent, East-Flanders, Belgium, c. 1900's*
Traditionally, genever is poured from a handcrafted
clay bottle into small glassware.

Genever is a great way to start an evening or just spend some time chatting with friends. A versatile drink, genever can be enjoyed as an aperitif, digestive, or after-dinner drink, and even has gastronomic possibilities.

Growing up, my parents had a restaurant named De Waterhoeve. The restaurant seated 150 people, providing an upscale dining experience that easily lasted 3-4 hours. Just before the entrée of a five-course menu paired with wine, customers were served young genever, neat, as a digestive. To keep the genever cold and give it a more attractive, upscale packaging, my parents placed a tall shot glass inside a large cognac glass filled ¾ with crushed ice and then poured chilled young genever into the shot glass. To keep the glasses from freezing to the ice, both glasses were served at room temperature. It was not unusual for customers to order an additional old genever with dessert as an after-dinner drink.

Fish and cheese pair very well with genever. The Netherlands' most characteristic drink pairs best with the country's most characteristic dish: *haring* (herring). Tradition may dictate that you have vodka with caviar, champagne with oysters, sake with sushi, beer with mussels, or wine with cheese, but these are all good reasons to get (re)acquainted with genever and surprise your taste buds! Side by side with any meat, particularly wild poultry and game, genever shines too, especially when incorporated as an ingredient into the dish.

# Confit Duck Leg
# with Red Currant Genever Glaze

*Created by Chef Claudio Pirollo, named*
*"Best Young Chef in Belgium"*

## Ingredients (Serves 4):
4 duck legs, skin on
2 lbs of duck fat
1 tablespoon thyme
2 bay leaves
½ tablespoon salt
1 shallot
1 large onion
4 garlic heads
2 carrots
500 ml (2 cups) wine
300 ml (1 ¼ cups) red currant genever
500 ml (2 cups) veal stock
8 large Portobello mushrooms
chives

## Preparation:
Soak the duck legs for 24 hours in their fat with thyme, bay leaves and salt. Refrigerate. The next day, preheat oven to 275 °F and cook legs in their fat for 5 hours until the skin gets crispy. Set aside. In the meantime, prepare the glaze.

In a large pot, slightly caramelize sliced onion, garlic and shallots. Pour the red wine, red currant genever, and veal stock in the pot. Simmer very slowly. Add carrot chunks and let it simmer until the glaze mixture reduces to half its original volume. Strain the vegetables and continue cooking the mixture over low heat until it becomes a glaze with a silky shiny color.

Clean the mushrooms, slice them thinly and sauté in oil. Drizzle the red currant glaze over the duck legs and serve hot with vegetables and some chives.

*Smakelijk!*

Genever makes the perfect cocktail, too. Around the 21st century in Belgium and the Netherlands, lounge bars became fashionable: modern and starkly decorated small to mid-sized establishments featuring cocktails, with an upscale and chill atmosphere. Because of the increase of these sorts of modern cafés to attract a younger and more trendy crowd, the amount and popularity of old fashioned brown bars, where spirits are traditionally served neat, decreases and the popularity of cocktails sets in. But aside from the occasional mix with Coca-Cola, seltzer, or juice, the art of mixing genever in Europe has only just begun.

Even the martini, which has become one of world's best-known mixed alcoholic beverages, still has a very different meaning in the traditional genever-consuming countries, which I learned when ordering my first drink in the US. The bar didn't have any genever so I ordered a martini instead. When you order a martini in the US, you will be served a cocktail made with gin and vermouth, and garnished with an olive or a lemon twist. Yet in Belgium and the Netherlands the martini still refers to the Italian vermouth brand, served neat or over ice.

Since my arrival in the US I've ordered many more American concoctions requiring more than the addition of just one other ingredient. I began to realize that in the right hands, these mixed drinks can become pure masterpieces. Cocktail makers with the rights hands and skills are called mixologists. They are the equivalent of the chefs from the haute cuisine.

I became intrigued by the martini and mixing vermouth with genever, although during the 19th century in America, genever already had an early place at the cocktail bar.

# GENEVER
# COCKTAILS

Many people don't realize that one of Manhattan's original drinks was genever. Dutch settlement in North America began with the founding of New Amsterdam in 1614. The settlers established themselves on the southern tip of Manhattan Island - what would later be the center of New York City. With these explorers came barrels of the Low Countries' native spirit. Europeans were consuming genever where skyscrapers would later stand and nearly 340 years before the rise of the Empire State Building.

The booze culture these Europeans first imported is buried in oceans of time and we often forget how Americans ended up imbibing the way they do today. By 1732, the British laid claim to all of the settlements from Maine to Georgia. Yet, genever could be found in countless taverns across the original thirteen colonies. The British weren't exporting their London-style "dry" spirit, which they called gin, to the new world en masse until after 1850.

*New Amsterdam c. 1664 (looking approximately North)*

When those colonies became the United States, it didn't take long for a new way of drinking to emerge for a new country - and it had a name. It was called a "cock-tail." The cocktail wasn't a broad term for any mixed glass of hooch in 1800. It was a very specific recipe like a martini, sour, flip, or julep. The origins of the word remain disputed. Yet, we know what was in one, thanks to an editor of a newspaper based out of Hudson, New York called *The Balance and Columbian Repository*. In 1806, this newspaper published the cocktail recipe in response to a reader's inquiry. The editor declared the cocktail to be "spirits of any kind, sugar, water, and bitters." If you were having a cocktail party in the early 1800s and all you had was genever, you might be making genever cocktails.

The craftiest barmen of the time were not content with simply making the 1806 cocktail recipe. Many added to the original formula or improved on it. Some added dashes of pastis, vermouth, or maraschino. They called them "fancy cocktails" or "improved cocktails." It wasn't long before those who had grown up with the original cocktail balked at these new-fangled drinks. From there, it wouldn't be hard to see a crabby old man belly-up to the bar in the 1850s demanding that the barkeep simply give him that "old fashioned" cocktail to which he's accustomed. Just as *jonge* (young) genever had its detractors with the *oude* (old) genever crowd, so did the cocktail. The drinks of this time generally took popular spirits and added ingredients to them to enhance the flavor.

Towards the end of the 19th century the cocktail culture was roaring. According to *Gin: A Global History* by Lesley Jacobs Solmonson, records indicate that genever was imported roughly five times more than gin. As such, many classic cocktails had been originally put into practice with genever as opposed to gin. Legendary 19th century American barman Jerry Thomas wrote *The Bar-Tender's Guide: How to Mix Drinks* or *The Bon-Vivant's Companion* in 1862. Harry Johnson in 1882 wrote *Bartender's Manual of How to Mix Drinks*. Both books are classics and were the first of their kind. Both books also used genever (or what they called Holland gin) alongside brandy, rum, and whisky in their recipes.

British gin or "Mother's Ruin" finally edged out genever in the hearts of American consumer thanks in part to the introduction of Prohibition, which began in 1920. During this time, the United States federal government maintained a ban on the sale, manufacture, and transportation of alcohol. The 18th Amendment might have been successful in reducing the amount of alcohol Americans imbibed across the country. However, it ignited a rash of widespread, underground, and organized criminal activity. Not only that, it kicked-off a wave of homemade booze. When you think about it, gin is relatively easy to make compared to other spirits. Infuse a neutral grain spirit like vodka with juniper berries and other flavorings or spices. No aging in charred wood barrels (in most cases). No burdensome mashing or fermentation. Naturally, gin became one of the easiest spirits to make during Prohibition. Make it well enough and people will pay you money for it. Generally, these gins were of poor quality and had a harsh taste. This reality helped give rise to the popularity of cocktails in which mixers served to disguise amateur distilling. The bartender's craft drifted towards covering bad liquor's taste, not necessarily enhancing it.

The repeal of Prohibition in 1933 brought an end to "The Noble Experiment" and the production of bootleg gin dropped accordingly. However, the damage to genever's popularity had been done. The American consumer no longer remembered the unique taste of this beautifully complex spirit. Gin had officially replaced it as a key player in the American cocktail scene. As a result, London dry gin has continued to dominate the United States market when it comes to botanically-infused spirits.

Finely crafted cocktails took on various forms throughout the decades after Prohibition. However, most of the American cocktail culture favored expediency over quality. The rise of mass produced mixers and artificial flavorings turned the cocktail craftsman into a blend of the soda-jerk and convenient store clerk. Bartenders rolled their eyes at the old-timer who dared to order an Old Fashioned. If the spirit couldn't be easily dumped into a glass with a mixer, it was presumed nobody wanted it.

In 1980, the owner of the swanky Rainbow Room in Manhattan's Rockefeller Center asked his young manager, Dale Degroff, to rethink the cocktail program. He wanted a bar that revived the practices of the 19th century. Degroff pulled it off. Disciples of his program, like Audrey Saunders, spun off to run their own cocktail bars, like The Pegu Club in Lower Manhattan. It would take more than ten years for Degroff's legacy to spread to other restaurateurs. It would take the mass information sharing on the internet to take those ideas one step further.

Up until today, common cocktails like martinis, gimlets, and negronis have called for London dry gin. It wasn't until the rise of the modern cocktail movement that American consumers began giving genever another look. As a new wave of craft bartenders have started dissecting the old recipes and looking for new spirits to employ in their cocktails, the popularity of genever has risen.

Genever of any terroir is ideal for cocktails. The *O'de Flander oude graanjenever* (a genuine East-Flemish old genever distilled from 100% grain) in particular is great in the aforementioned 1806 cocktail recipe. The ingredients of the cocktail and the pure grain taste of the O'de Flander terroir renders the drink's flavor as citrusy and bright. Little sugar is required to reach a desired sweetness thanks to the malt wine within the old genever. The aromas of cereal and malt attract the whiskey drinkers while the spice and complexity of the taste intrigues the gin drinkers.

The *jonge jenever* (young genever) terroir is great

as a substitute for vodka or gin. Its neutrality is palatable to the vodka drinker and serves as a welcomed substitute. Chilled, crisp and clear drinks like martinis, gibsons, and tonics definitely serve as a proper vehicle for this genever. Other cocktails, such as the Tom Collins, fizz, and gimlet also lend themselves well to the young genever. Even the simple equation of "sugar, water, and bitters" works magnificently with this terroir. The neutrality also acts as a fitting canvas for infusion with fruits, vegetables, or spices.

The *fruit jenever* (fruit genever) terroir can be a powerful additive to cocktails. If used properly and with the right product, these genevers can bring an entirely new level of flavor to a cocktail. Passion fruit genever and red currant genever can complement a particular season or slightly alter a guest's mood. This newer terroir is meant to attract a younger generation of drinkers but it can also serve as that warm handshake to consumers who have never had genever.

The cocktail revival that is under way, coupled with a renewed interest in genever, means that more American drinkers will be introduced to this long-forgotten liquor category. The end of this book is only the beginning of a dialogue about genever. To continue the conversation over a drink, I've included classic genever cocktail recipes that have withstood the test of time, plus genever cocktails that have been mixed up more recently. *Gezondheid!*

## CLASSIC GENEVER COCKTAILS

*Genever Cocktail*
2 oz old genever
1/2 oz sugar
3 dashes bitters
Stir over ice in an old fashioned glass.
Garnish with a lemon twist and a cherry.

*Fancy Genever Cocktail*
2 oz old genever
1 spoonful maraschino liqueur
1/2 oz gomme syrup
2 dashes aromatic bitters
Stir over ice in an old fashioned glass.
Garnish with a twist.

*Improved Genever Cocktail*
2 oz old genever
1 dash maraschino liqueur
1 dash absinthe
2 dashes aromatic bitters
Stir over ice in an old fashioned glass.
Garnish with a lemon twist.

*Genever Daisy*
2 oz old genever
1/2 oz orgeat syrup
1 spoonful maraschino liqueur
1/2 oz fresh squeezed lemon juice
Shake ingredients with ice. Strain into a chilled
cocktail glass. Top with sparkling water.

*Genever Fizz*
2 oz old genever
1 oz simple syrup
1 oz fresh squeezed lemon juice
1 egg white
Shake ingredients without ice until frothy then shake
with ice. Strain into a chilled collins glass.
Add sparkling water.
Serve with a straw. No garnish.

*Flemish Martinez*
1 1/2 oz old genever
1 1/2 oz sweet vermouth
1 spoonful maraschino liqueur
2 dashes orange bitters
Stir ingredients with ice.
Strain into a chilled cocktail glass.
Garnish with an orange twist.

# OLD GENEVER
# COCKTAILS

*Created with Diep9*
*O'de Flander 2 year old grain genever*
*35% ABV (70 proof)*

*The Oregonian*
2 oz old genever
0.5 oz cinnamon syrup
0.5 oz fresh orange juice
2 dashes Angostura bitters
Shake ingredients with ice.
Strain into a chilled cocktail glass.
Garnish with a cherry.

*Oude Fashioned*
2 oz old genever
0.5 oz simple syrup
3-4 dashes Angostura bitters
3-4 dashes orange bitters
Add genever, sugar, and bitters into an
old-fashioned glass. Add ice. Stir 40 times.
Garnish with orange zest.

*Antidotal Negroni*
1.5 oz old genever
0.5 oz Punt e Mes
0.5 oz St. Germain
1 dash orange bitters
Stir over ice in an old-fashioned glass.
Expel the orange twist oil in glass
before using as a garnish.

*Good Old Honey Bees*
2 oz old genever
0.5 oz honey syrup
1 spoonful fernet
1 mint sprig
Stir ingredients over ice in a highball glass.
Garnish with a sprig of mint.

*Boardwalk Pimm's Cup*
0.75 oz old genever
0.75 oz Pimms
0.5 oz Grand Marnier
0.5 oz fresh squeezed lime juice
0.25 oz pomegranate juice
1 tsp. Green Chartreuse
seltzer water
Shake first six ingredients over ice and pour
into a highball glass filled with ice.
Top with a splash of seltzer.
Garnish with a lime wedge.

## YOUNG GENEVER
## COCKTAILS

*Created with Diep9*
*O'de Flander young grain genever*
*35% ABV (70 proof)*

*Belgian 75*
1.5 oz young genever
0.75 oz fresh squeezed lemon juice
0.5 oz simple syrup
Brut Champagne
Shake first 3 ingredients over ice.
Pour into a champagne flute and top off with
Champagne. Garnish with a lemon twist.

*Up And Down The Mountain*
2 oz young genever
1.5 oz elderflower liqueur
0.75 oz fresh lime juice
2 oz ginger beer
Shake with ice and strain into a collins glass
with fresh ice. Add ginger beer.
Garnish with a lime wheel.

*Over The Rainbow*
2 oz young genever
0.75 oz Cointreau
0.5 oz fresh grapefruit juice
Shake and double strain over ice in a highball glass.
Garnish with a grapefruit or orange twist.

*Hipster*
3 oz young genever
1 oz dry vermouth
1-2 dashes orange bitters
Stir over ice and strain into a chilled cocktail glass.
Garnish with an orange twist.

*Arnold Palmer Meets Manneken Pis*
2 oz young genever
1 bar spoon Campari
0.5 oz lemon juice
0.75 oz strong green tea (or black tea)
2 dashes orange or citrus bitters
1 mint sprig
Shake over ice and strain into a rocks glass.
Shake mint sprig over drink to expel oils.

*Tip Of The Spear*
2 oz young genever
0.5 oz simple syrup
spoonful aquavit
3-4 dashes Peychaud's bitters
Stir ingredients with ice in a highball glass.
Garnish with a lemon twist.

*Flemish Cobbler*
2 oz young genever
0.5 oz orange curaçao
1 spoonful simple syrup
1 slice of orange
2 strawberries
3 blackberries
1 mint sprig
Muddle the orange slice, 1/2 of a strawberry,
and simple syrup in the bottom of a silver cup.
Add genever, curaçao and a pile of crushed ice.
Stir. Garnish with blackberries, remaining
strawberry sliced up and a sprig of mint.

*Spring Fling*
1.5 oz young genever
0.75 oz Eden Orleans Cider & Bitters
0.5 oz fresh lime juice
0.3 oz Sumptuous blackberry syrup
Shake ingredients with ice and
strain into chilled martini glass.
Garnish with a lime peel and blackberry.

*The Godmother of Stokerij De Moor*
2 oz young genever
0.75 oz amaretto
3 dashes black walnut bitters
Stir with ice and strain into a chilled cocktail glass.
Garnish with a cherry.

*Mackenzie's Honey Bees*
2 oz young genever
0.75 oz sweet vermouth
0.75 oz honey syrup
0.75 oz fresh lemon juice
3 oz soda water
Add ingredients to a collins glass with ice.
Stir lightly. Garnish with a slice of lemon.

*Sundown in Antwerp*
1.5 oz young genever
0.75 oz Lillet
0.25 oz St. Germain
0.75 oz grapefruit juice
0.5 oz agave nectar (or 0.75 oz simple syrup)
2 dashes grapefruit bitters
Shake over ice and pour into champagne flute or
cocktail glass. Garnish with a grapefruit twist.

*The Huntsman From Flanders*
1.5 oz young genever
0.5 oz Jamaican rum
1 oz sour mix
Shake with ice and strain into a
chilled cocktail glass. Garnish with 2 cherries.

## RED CURRANT GENEVER
## COCKTAILS

*Created with Diep9*
*all natural red currant genever*
*20% ABV (40 proof)*

*Diep Trouble*
1.5 oz red currant genever
0.5 oz St. Germain
Champagne
Pour genever and St. Germain into a coupe.
Top off with Champagne.
Garnish with a lemon twist.

*Vermont Goddess*
2 oz red currant genever
1 oz old genever
1 oz fresh squeezed lemon juice
1 tsp. Vermont maple syrup
Shake over ice and pour over ice in a rocks glass.
Garnish with red currants or a cherry.

*When in Belgium*
2 oz red currant genever
1 Kriek (cherry) beer
Combine in a chilled tulip-shaped beer glass.

*Delano's March*
2 oz red currant genever
0.5 oz Fernet Branca
0.5 oz fresh lime juice
0.5 oz spiced grenadine
2 dashes Angostura bitters
Shake and strain into a chilled cocktail glass.
Garnish with a sprig of mint.

*What's New Pussycat?*
2 oz red currant genever
0.5 oz elderflower liqueur
0.75 oz fresh lemon juice
3-4 dashes Peychaud's bitters
Shake ingredients with ice.
Strain into a chilled cocktail glass.
Garnish with red currants or a lemon twist.

*Red Barn, Black Crow*
1.5 oz red currant genever
0.5 oz rye whiskey
1 spoonful maraschino liqueur
3 dashes Angostura bitters
Stir ingredients with ice in a highball glass.
Garnish with a lemon twist and a cherry.

*Red-Nosed Reindeer*
0.5 oz red currant genever
1.5 oz Bärenjäger honey liqueur
Shake Bärenjäger over ice and
strain into a chilled tall shot glass.
Slowly top off with chilled genever.

*Tonic Twist*
2 oz red currant genever
2 oz gin
tonic water
Combine gin and tonic over ice in a rocks glass.
Slowly pour red currant genever into the center
of the drink. Garnish with a slice of lime.

*Silk & Lace*
1 oz red currant genever
0.5 oz fresh lemon juice
1 spoonful orange curaçao
3 oz sparkling wine
Shake ingredients with ice.
Strain into a chilled cocktail glass.
Garnish with an orange twist.

*The European Cougar*
1.5 oz red currant genever
0.5 oz Campari
0.5 oz orange curaçao
1 oz fresh orange juice
Shake ingredients with ice.
Strain into a chilled cocktail glass.
Garnish with an orange twist.

*White Flowers, Red Berries*
2 oz red currant genever
1.5 oz fresh grapefruit juice
0.5 oz fresh lemon juice
0.5 oz elderflower liqueur
Shake with ice.
Strain into a champagne coupe.
Garnish with a lemon twist.

## PASSION FRUIT GENEVER COCKTAILS

*Created with Diep9*
*all natural passion fruit genever*
*20% ABV (40 proof)*

*Calypso Flip*
0.75 oz passion fruit genever
1.5 oz Crusoe organic silver rum
0.5 oz simple syrup
0.25 oz fresh lemon juice
1 egg white
Dry shake ingredients. Then shake with ice.
Double strain into chilled old-fashioned glass (no ice).
Add 4-5 dots of Angostura bitters onto the perimeter of
the foam. Spin 4-5 times to give the bitters a
"hurricane" design on the foam.

*Passion Witte*
2 oz passion fruit genever
1 white Belgian beer
Combine in a chilled pint glass.
Garnish with an orange wedge.

*Passion Fruit Margarita*
2 oz passion fruit genever
1 oz tequila
1 oz lime juice
1 tsp. agave syrup
Shake over ice and strain into a margarita glass
filled with ice and rimmed with sugar and salt.
Garnish with a lime wedge.

*Fresh Obsession*
1.5 oz passion fruit genever
1.5 oz red currant genever
0.5 oz fresh lemon juice
0.5 oz elderflower liqueur
Shake with ice.
Strain into a champagne coupe.
Garnish with a lemon twist.

*Seal The Deal*
1.5 oz passion fruit genever
1 oz Smuggler's Notch vodka
0.5 oz sour mix
2 oz lemon/lime soda
Add ingredients to a highball glass filled with ice.
Roll mixture back and forth 3-4 times.
Garnish with a slice of orange.

*Out To Brunch*
1.5 oz passion fruit genever
Prosecco
splash of Cointreau
Pour genever into a champagne flute.
Top with Prosecco and a splash of Cointreau.
Garnish with an orange twist.

*Passion Till Sunrise*
2 oz passion fruit genever
1 oz orange juice
splash of lemon juice
0.5 oz Cointreau
0.5 oz grenadine
Shake first 4 ingredients over ice and strain
into a martini glass. Slowly pour grenadine
around the inside edge of the glass.
Garnish with a sage leaf.

*Belgian Blonde Sangria*
1 ½ cups passion fruit genever
1 btl. Pinot Grigio or other dry white wine
¼ cup white cranberry juice
¼ cup pineapple juice
1 cup diced pineapple
1 lemon, cut into wheels
1 orange, cut into wheels
Combine genever, wine, and juice in pitcher.
Add fruit. Chill and serve.

*Pennsylvania Hill*
1.5 oz passion fruit genever
1.5 oz aged rum
0.5 oz fresh lemon juice
0.5 oz Demerara syrup
1 spoonful amaretto
Shake ingredients with ice.
Strain into a highball glass over fresh ice.
Garnish with a lemon twist and a cherry.

*Belgian Flotilla Grog*
1 oz passion fruit genever
1 oz Demerara rum
0.75 oz fresh lime juice
0.5 oz simple syrup
2-3 dashes Jerry Thomas' decanter bitters
Shake ingredients with ice.
Strain into a tiki tumbler with crushed ice.
Garnish with freshly grated nutmeg.

*3G Cocktail*
1.5 oz passion fruit genever
1 oz young genever
0.5 oz St. Germain
0.5 oz fresh squeezed lemon juice
Shake over ice and strain into a martini glass.
Garnish with a lemon twist.

*Fizz-Ical Attraction*
0.75 oz passion fruit genever
1.5 oz cognac
0.5 oz fresh lemon juice
0.5 oz simple syrup
3 dashes Peychaud's Bitters
1 oz egg white
3-4 oz soda water
Dry shake ingredients then shake with ice.
Strain into a chilled collins glass.
Add soda water.

# ACKNOWLEDGEMENTS

With special thanks to Davy Jacobs, the curator of the National Genever Museum in Hasselt, Belgium for helping me in my research; to Anthony Rivera, a Washington DC-based writer and mixologist for helping me in the research and creation of genever cocktails; and to my husband, family, and friends for their continuous support in my quest to share my beloved spirit, genever, with people in the United States and beyond.

I wish to express my thanks to the following sources of illustrative material and/or permission to reproduce it: National Genever Museum Hasselt, Flanders, Belgium: pp. 6, 19, 36, 44, 45, 49, 50, 52, 53, 55, 58, 64, 65, 69, 79, 91, 97, 105; National Genever Museum Schiedam, Holland, the Netherlands: pp. 28, 66, 90, 101; Author's collection: pp. 1, 5, 7, 23, 35, 40, 41, 57, 67, 68 (top), 77 (bottom), 89, 95, 99, 109, 124, 131, 132, 135, 138, 145 (bottom) picture taken by

# BIBLIOGRAPHY

Prof. Dr. Eric Van Schoonenberghe (1996), *Jenever in de Lage Landen*. Stichting Kunstboek Brugge, België.

Stefaan van Laere (2005), *Jenever, van korrel tot borrel*. Uitgeverij Davidsfonds NV, Leuven, België.

Prof. Dr. Eric Van Schoonenberghe, Dr. Karolien De Clippel, Prof. Dr. Harry Snelders (2007), *De wijze en de dwaas. De Alchemist in woord en beeld*. Uitgeverij Van de Wiele, Brugge, België.

Willem Verstraaten (1994), *Jenever, over levenswater en foezenolie*. Poch Pockets, Utrecht, Nederland.

Prof. Dr. Eric Van Schoonenberghe, *Nationaal Jenever Museum Hasselt*. Drukkerij Haletra nv, Houthalen-Helchteren, België.

Ronald Ferket, Hugo Elsemans (1987), *Jenever, een Belgische belevenis*. Project, Antwerpen, België.

Ronald Ferket, Joris Creve (1996), *Jenever, een culinaire belevenis.* Berghmans Uitgevers, Antwerpen/Apeldoorn, België.

Ronald Ferket (2010), *25 gesmaakte jaren van De Vagant*. De Vagant, Antwerpen, België.

Evelien Dekens, Julie Debrauwere, Davy Jacobs (2008), *Pierre Le Buveur et Jean L'Abstinent.* Uitgeverij Van de Wiele, Brugge, België.

Prof. Dr. Eric van Schoonberghe, Paul Spapens, Peter Zwaal, Michaël Van Giel (2012), *Tersluiks. Alcoholsmokkel en sluikstokerij in de Lage Landen.* Uitgeverij Snoeck, Heule, België.

Joyce-Pinsel-Meijer (2009), *Jenevermuseum, Louter Reclame 100 jaar jenever affiches.* Artemis, Schiedam, Nederland.

Prof. Dr. S Groeneveld, Drs. H.L.PH. Leeuwenberg (2008), *De Tachtigjarige Oorlog. De Opstand in de Nederlanden.* Walburg Pers, Zutphen, Nederland.

Prof. Dr. Klein, Prof. Dr. Manning, Prof. Dr. de Vroede, Dr. Vos, Dr. D'Hoker (1982), *Onze Lage Landen de bewoners vanaf de ijstijd tot heden*. M&P Boeken Weert, Nederland.

Ewoud Sanders (1997), *Borrel Woordenboek 750 namen voor onzen glazen boterham.* Standaard Uitgeverij, Den Haag/Antwerpen, Nederland/België.

Prof. Dr. Eric Van Schoonenberghe (1999), *Genever (Gin): A spirit full of history, science and technology*. Universiteit Gent, België.

André Dominé (2008), *The ultimate guide to spirits & cocktails.* H.f.ullman, New York, United States.

Lesley Jacobs Solmonson (2012), *Gin, a global history.* Reaction Books, London, England.

Bob Emmons (2000), *The book of gins & vodkas.* Open Court, Chicago, United States.

Regan Gaz (2009), *The bartenders' gin compendium.* Bloomington, Indianapolis, United States.

The European Parliament (2008), *Regulation (EC) No 110/2008 of the European Parliament and of the Council of 15 January 2008.* Official Journal of the European Union.

David Wondrich (2007), *Imbibe!* Penguin, NY, United States.

Jerry Thomas (2009), *How to Mix Drinks or The Bon Vivant's Companion.* Soho Books, NY, United States.

# INDEX

# ABOUT THE AUTHOR

From her teenage years, Véronique Van Acker-Beittel, born and raised in East-Flanders, Belgium, has had a passion for her country's traditional spirit, genever. After college, Véronique relocated to the U.S. in 2002, starting a career in Trade and Marketing with Fortune 500 companies. Unable to find her beloved spirit in the U.S., Véronique quit her job in 2010 to found Flemish Lion LLC, America's first importing  company of Belgian genever. Véronique lives in Vermont with her husband Matthew, where they enjoy the simple things in life while drinking genever, one sip at the time.

Made in the USA
Charleston, SC
21 July 2013